COLLINS GEM
ANTIQUE
MARKS

COLLINS GEM
BIBLE
GUIDE

COLLINS GEM
Body
LANGUAGE

COLLINS GEM
CARD
Games

COLLIN
CRIC

DOGS

COLLINS GEM
FIRST AID

COLLINS GEM
INTERNET
Connect

COLLINS GEM
PREDICTING

COLLINS GEM
Ready
REFERENCE

COLLINS GEM
SHARKS

COLLINS GEM
WHALES
& DOLPHINS

COLLINS GEM
WHISKY

COLLINS GEM
WORD
PROCESSING

COLLINS GEM
Your PC

D0120671

COLLINS GEM

FOOTBALL

Mark Gonnella

Authenticator: David Barber

HarperCollins*Publishers*

All Pictures courtesy of Allsport/Hulton Getty except:
Bridgeman: 11. Christie's Images: 26, 56-57, 161 (t). Coloursport: 20,
24-25, 34, 51, 63, 72, 73 (t), 76 (all), 77 (t), 85, 96, 146-147, 190,
226-227. Empics: 33, 46, 47, 64, 74, 93, 156-157, 223. Image
Select/Ann Ronan: 23. Mary Evans: 12-13, 16-17, 18. Topham: 34,
69, 152-153, 208, 212-213, 230.
All illustrations courtesy of Foundry Arts.

HarperCollins Publishers
PO Box Glasgow G4 0NB

First published in 1999

Reprint 10 9 8 7 6 5 4 3 2 1

ISBN 0 00 472341-4

Created and produced by Flame Tree Publishing, part of
The Foundry Creative Media Co. Ltd
Crabtree Hall, Crabtree Lane, Fulham, London SW6 6TY

Special thanks to Jennifer Kenna and Simon Ray-Hills

Printed in Italy by Amadeus S.p.A.

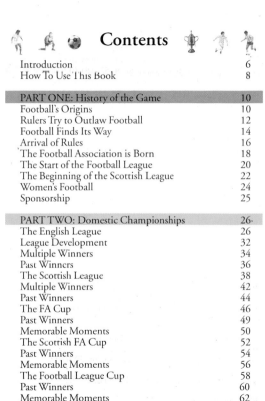

Contents

INTRODUCTION

THE DAY ANCIENT man first sampled the thrill of kicking a round object can be singled out as one of the defining events of our development.

From that fleeting moment has grown the world's most popular and recognised sport – FOOTBALL. It now pervades the hearts and minds of millions world-wide. It's a multi-billion pound industry, but above all else football is a game which rouses the passions like no other. One late, great manager claimed it is more important than life or death!

This book traces the game's origins and follows its development through the Victorian age to the modern spectacle of today. It looks at the history and records of major league competitions in England and Scotland as well as picking out some of the memorable moments from the FA Cup, League Cup, World Cup and European Cup competitions.

To provide an insight into the game's leading figures, selections are made of the best 20 players ever, the best 10 teams and the top 10 managers. For anyone looking to start playing the game, there are extensive tips on how to get fit and what skills and techniques are required. There is also advice for anyone with dreams of becoming a coach or referee.

For the armchair fan or player, we offer a simple guide to the rules of the game and explore and explain some of the tactics and formations employed by football managers. What is the WM formation, for example, and why do we have wing-backs or full-backs?

England win the World Cup in 1966.

These and many other questions will be answered in this book which aims to convey the drama, fun and emotion of what is universally known as 'the beautiful game'.

How To Use This Book

THIS BOOK CONTAINS all the essential information that is needed to play, and understand, the game of football. The origins of the game are explored, as is its current state. The most famous players, managers and incidents are recorded, and the backgrounds to the best-known competitions are looked at and the current statistics given. For those who would rather know how to play the game, and know what exactly the winger does and how to play like Michael Owen, there are three comprehensive instruction sections, detailing rules, techniques and tips for the would-be footballer or those returning to the sport. A plan of the pitch showing the various positions is a vital tool to the further understanding of the game; this is given in the instruction section. A good level of fitness means that the game can be more enjoyable; fitness tips for players of all ages are given.

Football is divided into eight sections, each one dealing with a different aspect of the game, with an extensive Glossary and Useful Address section at the end. Each section is colour coded for easy reference. Part One deals with the history of the Game, looking back to the origins of this game. Part Two looks at football in Britain: the competitions and winners. Parts Three and Four look at the European and international game: both at the nations that compete and at European and international competitions. Part Five details the best players and managers both past and present. Part Six is a guide to the laws of the game: what determines offside, the duration of a match and penalties. Part Seven looks at playing the game: where to play, tips on aspects of the game such as ball control, dribbling and goalkeeping, and Part Eight gives tips on tactics and formations.

The Glossary is a useful summary of terms used in the book and the Useful Addresses section contains advice on where to go for more information about all aspects of the game, such as the Football Association. A comprehensive index will lead to you to the relevant information contained in the book.

A The page number appears in a colour-coded box indicating which part of the book you are looking at.

B The aspect of the sport being dealt with is indicated at the head of the appropriate page.

C Instructive, interesting text gives all the essential information needed for the particular aspect of the sport.

D The topic covered on the page will be illustrated with clear photographs or diagrams, with identifying captions where appropriate.

HISTORY OF THE GAME

Football's Origins

The precise origins of association football remain
unknown, but the earliest records of man kicking
something resembling a ball date back to the Chinese
Han Dynasty of 2,000 years ago.

THE ANCIENT GREEKS and Romans developed the
pastime of *harpastum*, a strange mixture of association and
rugby football, which saw two teams engage in a battle to carry
a ball over a line marked at either end of a field.

It was the Romans, and Julius Caesar in particular, who
brought the game of *harpastum* to Britain, but it was during
the Middle Ages that the game really took a hold of the public.

Annual Shrovetide matches developed, played between two
teams of unlimited numbers, often from neighbouring villages.

Starting in a muddy market-place, the object of the game
was to propel a ball into the opposing side's goal. Rules were
non-existent and the matches were long, loud and violent.
Some players were trampled to death in the stampede towards
a rival goal.

The 'ball' was usually a pig's bladder, although historians
have recorded one infamous occasion in Chester when the
head of a Danish soldier was used as locals celebrated victory
over the invading Vikings.

The victorious side was the one which succeeded in grounding the ball in the opponents' goal. The player responsible was treated like a conquering hero and often carried back into town by his cheering companions.

During the fourteenth century the Japanese developed a game called *kenatt* which has many similarities with football.

An early game of football in Italy.

Rulers Try to Outlaw Football

Street matches were so popular in London during the Middle Ages that traders called on King Edward II to outlaw the game from the city.

FOOTBALL'S FIRST BAN was thus imposed on 13 April 1314, when Edward II outlawed football from London's streets decreeing: 'Forasmuch as there is great noise in the city caused by hustling over large balls, from which many evils arise, which God forbid; we command and forbid on behalf of the King, on pain of imprisonment, such game to be used in

the city in future.'

Football's position as the game of the people was affirmed again in 1349, when King Edward III tried to stop the game being played by young men whom he feared were spending more time playing football than practising the more noble and much-needed arts of archery and javelin throwing. Future monarchs Richard II, Henry IV and James III all made attempts to restrict the growth of 'such idle practices' without any real success.

Despite being frowned upon by the authorities, the game, which still resembled an unruly street chase after a ball, continued to blossom in towns and villages around Britain.

Oliver Cromwell did his best to stamp out the game and succeeded to some degree, with the game briefly disappearing before bursting back into life following the Restoration in 1660.

An early international game between England and Scotland.

He wrote: 'The ball, which is commonly made of blown bladder and cased with leather, is delivered in the midst of the ground, and the object of each party is to drive it through the goal of their antagonists, which being achieved, the game is won.'

In that aim, the game has remained unchanged throughout the years.

Preparing for a game of football in Elizabethan times.

Arrival of Rules

Having survived the various Royal attempts to outlaw the game during the Middle Ages, football remained a fairly lawless and unruly pastime until the mid-1840s. By that time the game was being played not only by the working man but also by young members of the modern establishment studying at the country's public schools and Oxford and Cambridge universities.

RULES WERE SET down differently by every school or club. Some allowed the ball to be handled, others did not. Many, though not all, outlawed hacking and tripping, and some restricted the numbers allowed on each side. As schools and clubs wanted to compete against each other, the lack of a unified set of rules and regulations was brought into sharp

focus. So, in 1848 two football players from Cambridge University, Messrs H. de Winton and J. C. Thring, called a meeting, with representatives from the major public schools to standardise how the game should be played. A meeting, lasting seven hours 55 minutes, produced the first formal set of rules for the game of association football.

Oxford vs. Cambridge; in the 1840s, schools and universities had their own rules for the game.

The Football Association is Born

> Sheffield FC, the world's oldest club, came into existence in 1855, while Notts County, the world's oldest league club, was formed in 1862.

AS MORE AND more clubs set up, the Football Association (FA) was formed, in October 1863, to administer the game, following a meeting at the Freemasons' Tavern, Great Queen Street, London. Eleven founder members were present and Mr A. Pember was appointed president.

C. W. Alcock.

Public schools including Harrow, Charterhouse and Westminster were initially reluctant to drop their own rules, but after some persuasion they agreed, and the first FA rules were published in December that year – not without some acrimony, however. Disagreements over the rules led to a split between the Associationists and the Rugby Unionists, the latter leaving the FA to develop their own game.

By 1880, 128 clubs and associations had joined the Football Association, run by secretary C. W. Alcock. There were 80 from the south of England, 41 from the north, six from Scotland and one from Australia.

It is not clear precisely when football arrived in Scotland, although the historical record states that one of the first clubs

Everton, Burnley, Accrington, Blackburn Rovers, Aston Villa, West Bromwich Albion, Wolverhampton Wanderers, Notts County, Derby County and Stoke. No clubs from the south were invited as they had not turned professional.

McGregor was duly appointed as the first League President and all sides were obliged to play their strongest teams in all matches.

The Football League kicked off on 8 September 1888 with Preston's Jack Gordon being credited with the first goal. It was the first of many records for Preston who were dubbed the 'Old Invincibles' after winning their first League Championship without losing a match and landing the FA Cup without conceding a goal.

1889 FA Cup winners, Preston North End.

The Beginning of the Scottish League

The Scottish League was formed in 1890 in response to the success of the English League, which was laying claim to some of the game's best players north of the border.

THE SCOTTISH GAME was still dominated at this time by Queen's Park who fervently opposed professionalism and wanted football to remain an amateur sport.

Rangers, Celtic, Third Lanark, Hearts, St Mirren, Dumbarton, Renton, Cowlairs, Cambuslang, Vale of Leven and Abercorn duly formed the Scottish League despite the protests of Queen's Park.

In a thrilling first season, the championship was shared for the one and only time, as Dumbarton and Rangers tied at the top of the table with 29 points apiece.

The Scottish League Cup.

Scotland vs. England, 1898.

At this stage Scottish football was regarded as superior to that of England. While English players tended to run with the ball until they lost possession, the Scots were the first to develop a passing game. They won 14 and drew six of the first 29 matches against their old foe.

Women's Football

Women's football did not come into being in any organised way until the 1960s, when clubs began springing up around the country. Since then the women's game has taken off all over the world. Girls are encouraged to play the game as much as boys, although mixed matches are not allowed above the age of 11.

SOME OF THE major English clubs have women teams playing in a national women's league. The most successful women's football team throughout the years have been the

Doncaster Belles who have a string of championship titles to their credit.

The first women's international to be played in Britain was between England and Scotland in 1972. England won 3-2. The first women's world championship was introduced in 1991 with the United States landing the title. No British team took part.

Arsenal Ladies vs. Liverpool Ladies, 1997.

Sponsorship

Until the 1970s football in Britain had failed to fulfil its true money-making potential. Advertising boards were at every ground but the thought of sponsorship by big business had not entered the equation.

THE DAY CLUBS first attracted sponsorship from major companies was the moment football really became an international business. It began with company names on team shirts but has now spread to league and cup competitions with major brand names fighting to land multi-million pound deals to have their name associated with football.

Television has also helped raise the game's profile and value, and in recent years a number of clubs have been floated on the Stock Exchange. When Manchester United floated in 1991, their assets were put at £39.9 million, proof, if it were needed, that football had come a long way in the 20th century.

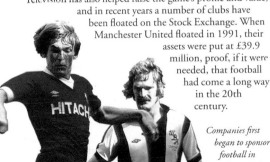

Companies first began to sponsor football in the 1970s.

DOMESTIC CHAMPIONSHIPS

The English League

Thanks to William McGregor's foresight in 1888, the League Championship quickly became established as the major competition for English football clubs.

THE EARLY YEARS

WITHIN FOUR YEARS, the initial league of 12 clubs had grown to two divisions consisting of 28 clubs. New grounds were built to cater for spectators who quickly pinned their colours to their home teams.

For the first four seasons all the teams came from the north. Preston North End's 'Old Invincibles' were the team to beat as they won the title in four successive years and were runners-up three times.

It was not until 1893 that Woolwich Arsenal became the first southern-based side to take part in the league. Within a year 32 teams were entered for the competition, and promotion and relegation were introduced in 1898.

Above: Football League medals. Right: The Football League trophies.

BETWEEN THE WARS

THE LEAGUE RAN continuously until the First World War brought the competition to a halt. Within two years of the end of hostilities in 1918, football was enjoying such growth that a third division was formed, taking the number of sides in the competition to 66.

In 1921 the League took on a form it very much resembles today, with four divisions operating for the first time. Two third divisions were founded with sides north of Birmingham going into the northern section and the others into the southern section. By 1923 there were 88 sides competing.

The Second World War forced the competition to be suspended in 1939 but after its return in August 1946, the League enjoyed a golden era.

THE GOLDEN ERA

WAR-WEARY supporters flocked to the country's football grounds, and in the 1948–49 season 41,271,414 people attended Football League matches.

In 1958 the League abandoned the regionalised Division Threes and formed a fourth division from the bottom 12 teams in each section. The move was the subject of much controversy at the time because of the increased costs for smaller clubs that resulted. The changed proved to be permanent, however, and the format is still in operation today.

THE SIXTIES

TOTTENHAM HOTSPUR began the 1960s by becoming the first team this century to clinch the League and Cup double, but the decade will always be remembered for the exploits of Manchester United. As a result of the Munich disaster in 1958, the club had a special place in people's hearts, and when Matt Busby led them to title wins in 1965 and 1967 the nation revelled in their success.

LIVERPOOL DOMINATE THE SEVENTIES

IF MANCHESTER UNITED won the plaudits in the 1960s, then their arch-rivals Liverpool will always be remembered as the team of the 1970s. Under Bill Shankly and then Bob Paisley, they won the League four times and were runners-up three times in seven years. On top of that they became the first British club to successfully win and defend the European Cup.

Left: Tottenham Hotspur, League Champions in 1961.

MERSEY RULE AND CHANGE

IN THE 1980s it was a familiar story on the pitch as Liverpool took the title five times. Indeed Merseyside became the Championship's permanent home, as Everton took the title on the two occasions their neighbours from the other side of Stanley Park missed out.

Major change arrived in 1987 when end of season play-offs were introduced for the first time. The final promotion and relegation places between the divisions were decided by sudden-death matches by which the top two or bottom two clubs were automatically promoted or relegated. There was considerable opposition from those who thought it unfair to add a final hurdle to a competition which had been contested over 46 games. However, they have helped produce some thrilling end of season matches and are now here to stay.

The Liverpool team in 1983.

INTO THE NEXT CENTURY

THE BIGGEST shake-up of the Football League since its birth came in 1992 when the country's top clubs joined forces to form the FA Premiership. Amid much acrimony and claims that smaller clubs would be driven out of business, the top 22 clubs in the land broke away from the auspices of the Football League.

It has resulted in unprecedented interest in the game. Attendances are at record levels, big business and TV companies are pouring in money. The Premier League is attracting major international stars and it is currently regarded as one of the most attractive leagues in which to play anywhere in the world.

Above: TV companies are constantly vying for coverage of the sport's major fixtures.

League Development

The table below shows how the League has developed
from its small beginnings.

DIVISIONS

Year	One	Two	Three (S)	Three (N)	Total
1888–91	12				12
1891–92	14				14
1892–93	16	12			28
1893–94	16	15			31
1894–98	16	16			32
1898–05	18	18			36
1905–15	20	20			40
1919–20	22	22			44
1920–21	22	22	22*		66
1921–23	22	22	22	20	86
1923–50	22	22	22	22	88
1950–87	22	22	24**	24**	92
1987–88	21	23	24	24	92
1988–91	20	24	24	24	92
1991–95*	22	24	24	22	92
1992–present	20***	24	24	24	92

*   Division Three

**   In 1958 clubs in Division Three (South) and Division
       Three (North) were reformed as Divisions
       Three and Four

*** In 1992 the Premier League came into being,
       with Divisions One, Two and Three below it.

The Football League Division Three trophy.

Multiple Winners

There have been many teams with remarkable League achievements, too many to list here, but below are some of the most remarkable.

ARSENAL

AFTER A successful period with Huddersfield, Herbert Chapman's magic touch took Arsenal to a Championship hat-trick between 1932–35. The 'Gunners' have gone on to lift the title 11 times. They won the League and FA Cup double in 1971 and became the second club to repeat the feat, in 1998.

Members of the winning Arsenal team in 1935.

HUDDERSFIELD TOWN

HUDDERSFIELD BECAME the first team to pull off a hat-trick of Championship victories. Revolutionary manager Herbert Chapman turned a team with little talent and resources into an irresistible force. He took over in 1921, leading them to their first title four years later. They repeated the feat the following season, and although Chapman moved to Arsenal in 1926, they won the race to the title.

Herbert Chapman.

MANCHESTER UNITED

MANCHESTER UNITED have won the title 12 times, their first success in 1908. They won the title twice during the 1960s during the Best, Law and Charlton era, but recently they have had five Championship successes in seven seasons under manager Alex Ferguson. In the 1998-99 season they won the League and Cup double, then made it the Treble with the European Championship.

PRESTON

PRESTON'S 'OLD INVINCIBLES' were the first true soccer power. In 1889 they won the first League Championship courtesy of a remarkable season in which they won 18 and drew four of their 22 matches. In the 1887–88 season, they also completed a record 26-0 first round FA Cup victory over Hyde. They retained the title the following season and were runners-up for the next three years.

Above: Manchester United: winners of the 1996 FA Cup Final.

Past Winners

LEAGUE CHAMPIONSHIP ROLL OF HONOUR

Year	Winners	Year	Winners
1947	Liverpool	1969	Leeds Utd
1948	Arsenal	1970	Everton
1949	Portsmouth	1971	Arsenal
1950	Portsmouth	1972	Derby County
1951	Tottenham Hotspur	1973	Liverpool
1952	Manchester Utd	1974	Leeds Utd
1953	Arsenal	1975	Derby County
1954	Wolverhampton Wanderers	1976	Liverpool
		1977	Liverpool
1955	Chelsea	1978	Nottingham Forest
1956	Manchester Utd	1979	Liverpool
1957	Manchester Utd	1980	Liverpool
1958	Wolverhampton Wanderers	1981	AstonVilla
1959	Wolverhampton Wanderers	1982	Liverpool
		1983	Liverpool
1960	Burnley	1984	Liverpool
1961	Tottenham Hotspur	1985	Everton
1962	Ipswich Town	1986	Liverpool
1963	Everton	1987	Everton
1964	Liverpool	1988	Liverpool
1965	Manchester Utd	1989	Arsenal
1966	Liverpool	1990	Liverpool
1967	Manchester Utd	1991	Arsenal
1968	Manchester City	1992	Leeds Utd

FA PREMIER LEAGUE ROLL OF HONOUR

Year	Winners	Year	Winners
1993	Manchester Utd	1997	Manchester Utd
1994	Manchester Utd	1998	Arsenal
1995	Blackburn Rovers	1999	Manchester Utd
1996	Manchester Utd		

Top: The Arsenal team who won the League and Cup double in 1998.
Bottom: Leeds United, who won the League Championship in 1969.

The Scottish League

Eleven Scottish clubs contested the very first Scottish League Championship in 1890 and for the one and only time it finished in a tie with Dumbarton and Rangers both ending up on 29 points. The trophy was shared, but the following season Dumbarton won it outright after pipping Celtic to the top spot by two points.

THE EARLY YEARS

FOR THE FIRST THREE years, professionalism was frowned upon by the Scottish FA but due to the pressure of players being lured away to English League clubs, they finally relented.

From the very beginning it was clear that the power in Scottish football would lie in Glasgow. Rangers and Celtic were runners-up in the first two competitions before Celtic began a monopoly in 1893, which has seen the two Glasgow giants dominate the game for more than a century. Such has been their supremacy that one or other of the two clubs has finished in the top two in every season bar five.

The Scottish Second Division was formed in 1893.

Left: the Celtic team. Above: the Scottish League trophy.

INTO THE TWENTIETH CENTURY

RANGERS AND CELTIC took a grip of the title race after Hibernian and then Third Lanark had the temerity to win the Championship in 1903 and 1904. In an unbroken run stretching 27 years, Rangers landed 14 title wins while Celtic collected 13. In total, just nine clubs other than the Glasgow giants have lifted the coveted Championship trophy. Aberdeen, Hearts and Hibernian have all won it four times. Rangers have a record 47 titles to their credit while Celtic have 36.

The Second Division was suspended during the First World War and did not resume until 1921. A Third Division made a brief appearance in 1923 but was dropped three years later.

After the game was suspended during the Second World War, the divisions were split into 'A', 'B' and 'C'. They were restored as the First and Second Divisions in 1956.

Rangers celebrate their championship victory.

PREMIER LEAGUE DAWNS

THE BIGGEST UPHEAVAL to the game north of the border came in 1975 in the shape of the Premier League. Partly due to pressure from Celtic and Rangers, who claimed that the existing league was becoming uncompetitive, the Premier Division was established, reduced in size to 10 clubs, with a First and Second Division of 14 sides each. It was a controversial move which prompted fears that smaller clubs would go out of business. That did not happen and meanwhile the status quo was quickly restored in Championship terms as Rangers collected the first Premier League title.

Celtic vs. Rangers in the Scottish Premier League.

Multiple Winners

CELTIC

CELTIC HAVE WON the League Championship 36 times. They won it first in 1893, the third season of the competition. Celtic completed the first 'double' of League Championship and FA Cup in 1907 and pulled off a clean sweep of trophies in 1967 when they won the League, FA Cup, Scottish League Cup and European Cup. From 13 November 1915 to 21 April 1917 they went unbeaten for a record 62 league matches. They have rarely been out of the top three since the Championship began and between 1966 and 1974 reeled off nine successive title wins. Their victory in the 1998 title race prevented their arch rivals Rangers beating that remarkable run.

Above: Celtic celebrate their 1998 title victory.

RANGERS

RANGERS HAVE 47 League Championship titles to their credit which is the best domestic performance of any club side. They shared the first trophy after tying with Dumbarton, and surprisingly took until 1899 to land their first title. In that season they became the first and only British club to win all of its league fixtures. In 1949 Rangers were the first Scottish club to pull off the treble of League, FA Cup and League Cup. They have repeated the feat four more times. In recent years they have even overshadowed Celtic by winning the title nine years in succession. That run only came to an end in 1998.

Rangers achieve victory over St Mirren in 1992.

Past Winners

SCOTTISH LEAGUE CHAMPIONSHIP
ROLL OF HONOUR

Year	Winners	Year	Winners
1947	Rangers	1962	Dundee
1948	Hibernian	1963	Rangers
1949	Rangers	1964	Rangers
1950	Rangers	1965	Kilmarnock
1951	Hibernian	1966	Celtic
1952	Hibernian	1967	Celtic
1953	Rangers	1968	Celtic
1954	Celtic	1969	Celtic
1955	Aberdeen	1970	Celtic
1956	Rangers	1971	Celtic
1957	Rangers	1972	Celtic
1958	Hearts	1973	Celtic
1959	Rangers	1974	Celtic
1960	Hearts	1975	Rangers
1961	Rangers		

SCOTTISH PREMIER DIVISION
ROLL OF HONOUR

Year	Winners	Year	Winners
1976	Rangers	1988	Celtic
1977	Celtic	1989	Rangers
1978	Rangers	1990	Rangers
1979	Celtic	1991	Rangers
1980	Aberdeen	1992	Rangers
1981	Celtic	1993	Rangers
1982	Celtic	1994	Rangers
1983	Dundee Utd	1995	Rangers
1984	Aberdeen	1996	Rangers
1985	Aberdeen	1997	Rangers
1986	Celtic	1998	Celtic
1987	Rangers	1999	Rangers

Scottish League Cup Champions Rangers.

The FA Cup

Football Association secretary C. W. Alcock's dream of a knockout cup competition for the country's football teams way back in 1871 must go down as one of the great flashes of sporting inspiration.

BACKGROUND

THAT MOVE has spawned thousands of similar competitions around the world, but it is the English FA Cup which has the ability to provoke emotions and reactions like no other.

Ironically, Alcock was captain of the Wanderers side which won the first competition, with a 1-0 victory over the Royal Engineers at the Kennington Oval on 16 March 1872. Just 15 teams had entered.

It is now an eight-month long marathon, open to clubs affiliated to the Football Association. Pre-qualifying rounds between non-league

Left: the FA Cup.
Right: Yeovil Town vs. Arsenal, 1993.

teams start in September for the right to go into the first round, where they are joined by professional sides from the Second and Third Divisions.

Clubs from the top division and the Premier League join the fray for the third round and it is often at this stage that the competition creates its biggest dramas. Millionaire internationals can suddenly find themselves playing at tiny grounds against talented part-timers looking to perform a giant-killing act before returning to their daily labours in business and industry.

Whatever their background, all players dream of reaching the May final at Wembley, which has hosted the game's showpiece fixture since 1923. With a pomp and ceremony unique to Britain, the game is attended by royalty and has become an essential start to the English sporting summer.

THE FA CUP TROPHY

THERE HAVE BEEN four FA Cup trophies during the competition's long history. The first trophy was stolen from a Birmingham shop in 1895 where it was on display following Aston Villa's victory. The second was presented to Lord Kinnaird in recognition of his service to the FA in 1910, while the third was replaced in 1992 after 81 years of service.

Above: the original FA Cup trophy.

Past Winners

Year	Winners	Year	Winners
1946	Derby County	1972	Leeds Utd
1947	Charlton Athletic	1973	Sunderland
1948	Manchester Utd	1974	Liverpool
1949	Wolverhampton Wanderers	1975	West Ham Utd
1950	Arsenal	1976	Southampton
1951	Newcastle Utd	1977	Manchester Utd
1952	Newcastle Utd	1978	Ipswich Town
1953	Blackpool	1979	Arsenal
1954	West Bromwich Albion	1980	West Ham Utd
1955	Newcastle Utd	1981	Tottenham Hotspur
1956	Manchester City	1982	Tottenham Hotspur
1957	Aston Villa	1983	Manchester Utd
1958	Bolton Wanderers	1984	Everton
1959	Nottingham Forest	1985	Manchester Utd
1960	Wolverhampton Wanderers	1986	Liverpool
1961	Tottenham Hotspur	1987	Coventry City
1962	Tottenham Hotspur	1988	Wimbledon
1963	Manchester Utd	1989	Liverpool
1964	West Ham Utd	1990	Manchester Utd
1965	Liverpool	1991	Tottenham Hotspur
1966	Everton	1992	Liverpool
1967	Tottenham Hotspur	1993	Arsenal
1968	West Bromwich Albion	1994	Manchester Utd
1969	Manchester City	1995	Everton
1970	Chelsea	1996	Manchester Utd
1971	Arsenal	1997	Chelsea
		1998	Arsenal
		1999	Manchester Utd

Left: the Arsenal team that won the 1971 FA Cup Final.

Memorable Moments

THE WHITE HORSE FINAL

THE FIRST FA CUP Final to be staged at Wembley, 28 April 1923, is remembered for the heroics of a police constable who rode a white horse in an effort to control crowds swarming on to the pitch before the match between Bolton Wanderers and West Ham United. PC George Scorey and his horse Billy were

hailed as heroes, as an estimated 250,000 people packed into the stadium for a match which saw Bolton triumph 2-0.

RECORD 10 FOR UNITED

MANCHESTER United have won the FA Cup a record 10 times. Their first success came in the 1909 final when they beat Bristol City 1-0. Tottenham Hotspur are the next most successful Cup side, with eight victories to their credit, while Aston Villa and Arsenal have landed the trophy seven times.

PC George Scorey and Billy at the White Horse Final.

THE MATTHEWS' FINAL

STANLEY MATTHEWS had twice been an FA Cup Final loser when he arrived at Wembley with his Blackpool side in 1953 to face Bolton Wanderers. When Matthews' side trailed 3-1 after 55 minutes all looked lost. In an inspirational display down the right wing, he set up two goals. Stan Mortensen bagged a hat-trick in the process and Blackpool had produced one of the all-time FA Cup comebacks, winning 4-3.

GIANT-KILLING ACTS

THE FA CUP HAS seen some of the biggest upsets of any soccer competition. Non-league Yeovil have the most impressive giant-killing record, beating league opponents 17 times. Smaller league clubs have also pulled off some heroic feats. One of the biggest upsets came in 1933 when Third-Division Walsall beat Herbert Chapman's great Arsenal side 2-0.

Above: Third-Division Walsall celebrates their victory over Arsenal, 1933.

The Scottish FA Cup

The Scottish FA Cup came into existence on 13 March 1873, when eight clubs attended a meeting called by Queen's Park to found the Scottish FA.

THE EARLY YEARS

WITH A BANK balance of just £1 11s 4d in its first year, the Scottish FA asked for donations from its 16 member clubs to pay for the trophy and badges which cost £56 12s 11d. Queen's Park, then regarded as the best team in the world, won the first final 2-0 against Clydesdale. They went on to win the cup for the first three years. Celtic have won the Cup a record 30 times.

Left: Celtic have won the Cup a record number of 30 times.
Above: the Scottish FA Cup trophy.

Past Winners

Year	Winners	Year	Winners
1947	Aberdeen	1973	Rangers
1948	Rangers	1974	Celtic
1949	Rangers	1975	Celtic
1950	Rangers	1976	Rangers
1951	Celtic	1977	Celtic
1952	Motherwell	1978	Rangers
1953	Rangers	1979	Rangers
1954	Celtic	1980	Celtic
1955	Clyde	1981	Rangers
1956	Hearts	1982	Aberdeen
1957	Falkirk	1983	Aberdeen
1958	Clyde	1984	Aberdeen
1959	St Mirren	1985	Celtic
1960	Rangers	1986	Aberdeen
1961	Dunfermline Athletic	1987	St Mirren
		1988	Celtic
1962	Rangers	1989	Celtic
1963	Rangers	1990	Aberdeen
1964	Rangers	1991	Motherwell
1965	Celtic	1992	Rangers
1966	Rangers	1993	Rangers
1967	Celtic	1994	Dundee Utd
1968	Dunfermline Athletic	1995	Celtic
		1996	Rangers
1969	Celtic	1997	Kilmarnock
1970	Aberdeen	1998	Hearts
1971	Celtic	1999	Rangers
1972	Celtic		

Celtic, who have won the Cup 15 times since 1947.

Memorable Moments

GOAL RECORD – 1885

IN THE FIRST ROUND of the FA Cup on 12 September 1885, Arbroath beat Bon Accord 36-0, a record for any British first-class match which still stands today. Bon Accord played the game in their working clothes and without a pair of football boots between them. Their injured goalkeeper was replaced with a half-back who had never been in goal before. Arbroath winger John Petrie scored a record 13 goals.

CROWD TROUBLE MARS 1909 FINAL

THE 1909 TROPHY was not awarded after the replayed final between Celtic and Rangers erupted into violence. When the match ended in a 1-1 draw, fans expected extra-time but the rules did not allow this. Spectators suspected a plot was afoot to make money by staging another match, and in the trouble that followed, 100 policemen and firemen were injured.

CELTIC LAND 1907 DOUBLE

CELTIC'S FINAL TRIUMPH over Hearts by a 3-0 scoreline meant they became the first club to do the League and Cup double north of the border. They were helped on their way by a controversial penalty from William Orr, the first time a goal had been scored from the spot in Cup Final history.

GIANT-KILLING BERWICK

LITTLE BERWICK RANGERS pulled off what was described as the 'shock of the century' as they beat Cup holders Rangers 1-0 in the first round of the 1966–67 competition. Berwick went ahead through Sammy Reid after 32 minutes. Their goalkeeper-manager, Jock Wallace, performed heroics to keep the Second Division side in front, and history was made.

Footballing caps from the turn of the century.

The Football League Cup

The League Cup did not come into being until the 1960–61 season. It was the brainchild of the then secretary of the Football League, Alan Hardaker, who saw it as a new source of income for the 92 League clubs. Five of the top clubs in the country refused to contest the first Cup because they felt that the competition overloaded an already crowded fixture list.

THE EARLY YEARS

IT WAS ORGANISED on a knockout basis, with a two-legged semi-final and final. It was only when the final moved to

Wembley that the competition grew in popularity. With a Fairs Cup (see p. 74) place also on offer to the winners, the competition's future was secure. In 1981 it became the first English football competition to be sponsored, when the National Dairy Council gave it their support. The Milk Cup, as it was then called, has since become the Littlewoods Cup and the Coca Cola Cup. In season 1998–99 it was known as the Worthington Cup.

Above: Swindon Town celebrate their League Cup victory, 1969.
Left: the Coca-Cola Cup, formerly known as the League Cup.

Past Winners

The Coca-Cola Cup.

THE LEAGUE CUP

Year	Winners
1961	Aston Villa
1962	Norwich City
1963	Birmingham City
1964	Leicester City
1965	Chelsea
1966	West Bromwich Albion
1967	Queens Park Rangers
1968	Leeds Utd
1969	Swindon Town
1970	Manchester City
1971	Tottenham Hotspur
1972	Stoke City
1973	Tottenham Hotspur
1974	Wolverhampton Wanderers
1975	Aston Villa
1976	Manchester City
1977	Aston Villa
1978	Nottingham Forest
1979	Nottingham Forest
1980	Wolverhampton Wanderers
1981	Liverpool

MILK CUP

Year	Winners
1982	Liverpool
1983	Liverpool
1984	Liverpool
1985	Norwich City
1986	Oxford Utd

LITTLEWOODS CUP

Year	Winners
1987	Arsenal
1988	Luton Town
1989	Nottingham Forest
1990	Nottingham Forest

RUMBELOWS CUP

Year	Winners
1991	Sheffield Wednesday
1992	Manchester Utd

COCA-COLA CUP

Year	Winners
1993	Arsenal
1994	Aston Villa
1995	Liverpool
1996	Aston Villa
1997	Leicester City
1998	Chelsea

WORTHINGTON CUP

Year	Winners
1999	Tottenham Hotspur

Memorable Moments

WEMBLEY FIRST FOR QPR

THE FIRST LEAGUE Cup final to be staged at Wembley in 1967 produced one of the most dramatic matches, as Third

Division Queen's Park Rangers came from two goals down to snatch victory against First-Division West Bromwich Albion. Rangers were outclassed in the first half but, thanks to the inspirational Rodney Marsh, scored three goals in the last half hour to seal a remarkable victory.

SWINDON'S JOLLY ROGERS

THIRD DIVISION Swindon's 3-1 extra-time victory over Arsenal in 1969 remains one of the competition's greatest upsets. Arsenal were the hot favourites and took control early on, but ten minutes before half-time a defensive mistake presented Swindon's Roger Smart with a simple tap-in. Bobby Gould equalised for a flu-hit Arsenal, with four minutes to go, but in extra-time Swindon winger Don Rogers took centre stage. He scored Swindon's second and then raced half the pitch to secure a third in spectacular style.

Third-Division Swindon beats the First-Division giants Arsenal, 1969.

LIVERPOOL'S FOUR IN A ROW

WHEN LIVERPOOL'S GRAEME SOUNESS cracked home a first-half goal in the replayed 1984 final against neighbours Everton, it gave the Reds an unprecedented fourth League Cup

victory in succession. They had won the competition for the first time in 1981, when they beat West Ham United 2-1 in a replay. They followed that by beating Tottenham Hotspur 3-1 in 1982, and had then gone on to beat Manchester United 2-1 in 1983. In total Liverpool have won the Cup five times, a record only equalled by Aston Villa, who won the very first competition.

Aston Villa, winners of the first League Cup Final in 1961.

EUROPEAN COMPETITIONS

Football in Europe

The British introduced football to Europe towards the end of the nineteenth century.

BACKGROUND

RECORDS SUGGEST English boys at a boarding school introduced a basic form of the game in Germany as early as 1865, while football was also popular in Austria, where there was a large British community in Vienna. Two English brothers who ran a mill near Moscow helped get the game going in Russia in 1887, while an English boy studying at a Danish public school is credited with introducing the game there.

It was not long before the Europeans had developed their own leagues and football was on its way to becoming the global game of today.

The Italian, Spanish, German, French and Dutch leagues are now among the best in the world.

Above: the European Cup.
Right: the world-famous Italian League Serie A, Bologna vs. Roma.

The European Cup

Former French international player and newspaper
editor Gabriel Hanot had the idea for the European
Champion Clubs' Cup after reading English newspaper
claims that Wolverhampton Wanderers were the
champions of the world due to friendly victories over
Moscow Spartak and Honved of Hungary.

THE EARLY YEARS

IN 1955 HANOT invited 20 leading European clubs to Paris
to discuss his idea, which was given rousing approval. The
competition involved the champions of each country playing
each other on a home and away basis, with the winners going

through to the next
stage on an aggregate
score. The final has
always been a one-off
match.

It has since
developed into the
Champions' League,
with the top three
clubs from major
European nations
fighting it out first on
a league then
knockout basis.

Real Madrid after their win in the 1998 Champions' League Final.

PAST WINNERS

Year	Winners	Year	Winners
1956	Real Madrid	1980	Nottingham Forest
1957	Real Madrid		
1958	Real Madrid	1981	Liverpool
1959	Real Madrid	1982	Aston Villa
1960	Real Madrid	1983	Hamburg
1961	Benfica	1984	Liverpool
1962	Benfica	1985	Juventus
1963	Milan	1986	Steaua Bucharest
1964	Internazionale	1987	Porto
1965	Internazionale	1988	PSV Eindhoven
1966	Real Madrid	1989	Milan
1967	Celtic	1990	Milan
1968	Manchester Utd	1991	Red Star Belgrade
1969	Milan		
1970	Feyenoord	1992	Barcelona
1971	Ajax	1993	Marseille
1972	Ajax	1994	Milan
1973	Ajax	1995	Ajax
1974	Bayern Munich	1996	Juventus
1975	Bayern Munich	1997	Borussia Dortmund
1976	Bayern Munich		
1977	Liverpool	1998	Real Madrid
1978	Liverpool	1999	Manchester Utd
1979	Nottingham Forest		

Memorable British Moments

1967

CELTIC BECAME THE first British club to win the European Cup when they triumphed 2-1 over Italy's Internazionale in Lisbon. After only eight minutes Mazzola scored from a penalty, but the Scots hit back with two second-half goals. The Scottish champions won the League title, FA Cup, League Cup and European Cup in the same season.

1968

MANCHESTER UNITED WERE the first English club to win the European Cup, courtesy of a 4-1 victory over Benfica at Wembley. After the Portuguese side equalised nine minutes before time, the enigmatic George Best put United back in front three minutes into extra-time before 19-year-old Brian Kidd and Bobby Charlton put the result beyond doubt.

Manchester United with the European Cup, 1968.

1977

LIVERPOOL MADE THEIR breakthrough at European Cup level with a convincing 3-1 victory over Borussia Munchengladbach. Midfielder Terry McDermott put the Reds in front after 28 minutes but Simonsen equalised early in the second half. Tommy Smith scored a rare goal before Phil Neal's penalty seven minutes from the end sealed victory.

1982

THE EUROPEAN CUP stayed in English hands for a record-breaking sixth year as Aston Villa pulled off a major upset by beating German champions Bayern Munich 1-0 in Rotterdam. Battling striker Peter Withe scored the all important goal after 67 minutes.

1985

LIVERPOOL'S FIFTH FINAL at Belgium's Heysel Stadium against Juventus will always be remembered for the sickening loss of 39 fans' lives. The supporters, mostly Italian, died when Liverpool followers charged at their rivals and a safety wall collapsed. Juventus won the match 1-0 but the trouble led to Liverpool being banned from European competitions indefinitely while all other English clubs were to be excluded for five years.

Plan of the Heysel Stadium in Brussels, showing where the disaster occurred.

European Cup-Winners' Cup

The competition began in the 1960–61 season and as the name suggests is for the national cup winners of European nations. Games are played on a home-and-away basis with a sudden-death final.

THE EARLY YEARS

IN THE FIRST competition, only 10 sides took part. This was largely due to the fact that in many continental countries, the national cup competition was very much the also-ran in comparison to the league championship. However, the first competition was such a success that the following year 23 countries entered and it has gone from strength to strength ever since.

PAST WINNERS

Year	Winners	Year	Winners
1961	Fiorentina	1980	Valencia
1962	Atletico Madrid	1981	Dynamo Tbilisi
1963	Tottenham Hotspur	1982	Barcelona
		1983	Aberdeen
1964	Sporting Lisbon	1984	Juventus
1965	West Ham Utd	1985	Everton
		1986	Dynamo Kiev
1966	Borussia Dortmund	1987	Ajax
		1988	Mechelen
1967	Bayern Munich	1989	Barcelona
1968	Milan	1990	Sampdoria
1969	Slovan Bratislava	1991	Manchester Utd
1970	Manchester City	1992	Werder Bremen
1971	Chelsea	1993	Parma
1972	Rangers	1994	Arsenal
1973	Milan	1995	Real Zaragoza
1974	Magdeburg	1996	Paris St Germain
1975	Dynamo Kiev	1997	Barcelona
1976	Anderlecht	1998	Chelsea
1977	Hamburg	1999	Lazio
1978	Anderlecht		
1979	Barcelona		

Tottenham Hotspur, winners of the 1963 European Cup-Winners' Cup.

Memorable British Moments

1963

TOTTENHAM HOTSPUR BECAME the first British side to lift a European trophy when they thrashed the existing cup-holders, Atletico Madrid of Spain, 5-1. Jimmy Greaves and Terry Dyson scored twice, while John White, who was tragically killed by lightning while playing golf a year later, scored the other.

1970

A GOAL FROM NEIL Young and a Francis Lee penalty gave Manchester City their first taste of European glory when they overcame Poland's Gornik Zabrze 2-1. City were left with an anxious final 20 minutes when the Poles pulled a goal back, but they held on to victory in front of a pitiful Vienna crowd of just 8,000.

Above: Manchester City, winners in 1970 after their defeat of Poland's Gornik Zabrzep. Top right: the victorious Rangers in 1972. Bottom right: Manchester United team members after their 2-1 victory over Barcelona, 1991.

1972

BRITISH DOMINANCE of the competition continued for a third successive year as Rangers overcame Moscow Dynamo in a five-goal thriller. The game was marred by a series of pitch invasions by Rangers' followers each time their side scored. Colin Stein, and Willie Johnston with two, fired the Scots 3-0 up after 49 minutes, but they nearly paid the price for relaxing when the Russians struck back with two late goals.

1991

MANCHESTER UNITED marked the return of English clubs to European competition following the Heysel Stadium tragedy with a magnificent victory over favourites Barcelona. Mark Hughes scored the goals which took United to a 2-1 success. Victory also marked a second Cup-Winners Cup success for manager Alex Ferguson who had been in charge of Aberdeen eight years earlier.

Fairs Cup/UEFA Cup

The oldest European club competition was instigated in 1955 on the suggestion of then UEFA vice-president, Ernst Thommen of Switzerland, who wanted to introduce some extra spice to friendly matches between cities staging trade fairs.

THE EARLY YEARS

ORIGINALLY NAMED the International Industries Fairs Inter-Cities Cup, the first competition was held over two seasons. Some cities were represented by teams selected from all clubs based within their area. The London side, for instance, was chosen from the 11 teams based within the capital.

From 1961 the three teams finishing below the champions were allowed from each country, although no one city could include more than one team. The competition was re-named the UEFA Cup in 1972 when this rule was lifted.

The UEFA Cup.

PAST WINNERS
Fairs Cup

Year	Winners	Year	Winners
1958	Barcelona	1966	Barcelona
1960	Barcelona	1967	Dynamo Zagreb
1961	Roma	1968	Leeds Utd
1962	Valencia	1969	Newcastle Utd
1963	Valencia	1970	Arsenal
1964	Real Zaragoza	1971	Leeds Utd
1965	Ferencvaros		

UEFA Cup

Year	Winners	Year	Winners
1972	Tottenham Hotspur	1985	Real Madrid
		1986	Real Madrid
1973	Liverpool	1987	IFK Gothenburg
1974	Feyenoord	1988	Bayer Leverkusen
1975	Borussia Munchengladbach	1989	Napoli
		1990	Juventus
1976	Liverpool	1991	Internazionale
1977	Juventus	1992	Ajax
1978	PSV Eindhoven	1993	Juventus
1979	Borussia Munchengladbach	1994	Internazionale
		1995	Parma
1980	Eintracht Frankfurt	1996	Bayern Munich
		1997	Schalke
1981	Ipswich Town	1998	Internazionale
1982	IFK Gothenburg	1999	Parma
1983	Anderlecht		
1984	Tottenham Hotspur		

Memorable British Moments

1968

LEEDS UNITED'S NARROW 1-0 win over Hungary's Ferencvaros was a sweet victory for the Elland Road club who had lost in the previous year's final to Dynamo Zagreb. A single Mick Jones goal gave Leeds the lead in the first leg and they fought out a goalless draw in Hungary to secure the trophy.

1970

ARSENAL MADE IT a hat-trick of English successes with a 4-3 triumph over Anderlecht of Belgium. The 'Gunners' were 3-1 down after the first leg, but staged a magnificent performance in the second leg at Highbury, which saw Eddie Kelly, John Radford and Jon Sammels score the goals to lift the Cup.

Top: Leeds United in 1968. Bottom: Arsenal in 1970.

1973

LIVERPOOL, WHO were to become a force in European cup football, collected their first international trophy and completed a remarkable six-year winning run for English clubs with a 3-2 aggregate win over Borussia Munchengladbach of Germany.

Liverpool's Kevin Keegan celebrating in 1973.

1981

IPSWICH SURVIVED a thrilling final against AZ 67 Alkmaar of Holland to emerge victorious by a 5-4 aggregate. The Suffolk side established a 3-0 lead in the first leg. The Dutch provided formidable opposition in the return and won the game 4-2, but Ipswich had done enough.

Mick Mills of Ipswich in 1981.

1984

YOUNG RESERVE TEAM goalkeeper Tony Parks was the hero as Spurs survived a nail-biting penalty shoot-out against Anderlecht. The two sides were deadlocked after drawing both legs 1-1, but Parks produced two fine saves in the penalty decider to give Spurs victory by a 4-3 margin.

Graham Roberts and Gary Mabbutt of Spurs, 1984.

THE WORLD CUP

The Early Years

Frenchman Jules Rimet is the man responsible for bringing the World Cup into being. Rimet was the President of FIFA in the early 1920s and suggested a competition involving the top soccer nations to find the best team in the world.

THE FIRST TOURNAMENT was staged in Uruguay in 1930. Just 13 countries – Uruguay, Argentina, Brazil, Paraguay, Peru, Chile, Mexico, Bolivia, United States, France, Belgium, Yugoslavia and Romania – entered. The Europeans were particularly reluctant to enter because they faced a three-week boat journey to reach the finals.

The sides were split into four groups and the first World Cup match saw France lose their goalkeeper through injury but still go on to beat Mexico 4-1. Uruguay were subsequently crowned the first World Champions after they beat Argentina 4-2 in the final.

The competition has since blossomed into one of the great showpiece sporting events, with teams entering from 172 nations around the globe for the 1998 competition. The host nations have won the competition six times in 16 tournaments.

Location of Finals and Past Winners

Location	Year	Winner
Uruguay	1930	Uruguay
Italy	1934	Italy
France	1938	Italy
Brazil	1950	Uruguay
Switzerland	1954	West Germany
Sweden	1958	Brazil
Chile	1962	Brazil
England	1966	England
Mexico	1970	Brazil
West Germany	1974	West Germany
Argentina	1978	Argentina
Spain	1982	Italy
Mexico	1986	Argentina
Italy	1990	West Germany
USA	1994	Brazil
France	1998	France
Japan/Korea	2002	

Left: Jules Rimet, founder of the World Cup.
Right: the Jules Rimet World Cup trophy.

Memorable Moments: England

England have flattered to deceive during most of the 10
World Cup finals they have contested. Victory in 1966
will always be the highlight, while more recently the
penalty shootout agonies of Italia 90 and France 98
remain imprinted on the memory. Below are some
of the highlights – and lowlights – of England's
World Cup campaigns.

ENGLAND 1966

A HAT-TRICK from West Ham United's Geoff Hurst fired Alf
Ramsey's England side to final glory in a thrilling 4-2 victory
over West Germany. England had reached the final at Wembley

after topping their opening group and defeating Argentina 1-0 in the quarter-finals and Portugal 2-1 in the semis, They looked in trouble in the final when the Germans went in front early on through Haller. Hurst equalised shortly afterwards and then Martin Peters put them ahead before Weber scrambled an equaliser near the end to force extra-time. The match turned on a controversial 100th-minute shot from Hurst which crashed off the crossbar and over the line – or not as the case may be. Hurst later put the issue beyond doubt by firing in his third of the game. It remains the only time a player has scored a hat-trick in a World Cup Final.

Above: Bobby Moore, captain of the victorious 1966 team.
Left: England 4, West Germany 2 – the host country celebrates.

MEXICO 1986

ENGLAND'S HOPES WERE SHATTERED in controversial
style in the quarter-final, courtesy of Diego Maradona's
infamous 'Hand of God' goal. TV pictures showed
conclusively that the brilliant Argentinian midfielder fisted
his team's opening goal past Peter Shilton, though his second
shortly afterwards, a jinking run which left four England
defenders sprawling, ranks as one of the finest goals ever to
grace the competition.

The infamous 'Hand of God' goal in 1986.

ITALY 1990

ENGLAND produced their best performance since winning the trophy by reaching the semi-finals. They scraped through the group matches by beating Egypt and drawing with the Republic of Ireland and Holland before knocking out Belgium in the second round with the last kick of the game. England overcame an impressive Cameroon 3-2 in the quarter-finals which took them to a semi-final showdown with West Germany. Extra-time failed to separate the two teams at 1-1 but in an agonising penalty shootout, Stuart Pearce and then Chris Waddle missed from the spot to shatter England's hopes of reaching the Final.

Stuart Pearce, after his crucial penalty miss in Italia 90.

Memorable Moments: Scotland

The Scots have qualified for eight World Cup finals. They have always travelled high on hope and expectation and with hordes of fanatical supporters. However, they have been bedevilled by ill luck and near misses, and have yet to reach the second stage of the competition.

WEST GERMANY 1974

SCOTLAND CLINCHED their first ever World Cup Final victory by beating Zaire 2-0 in their opening game in the West German tournament. In one of their best-ever displays, they went on to draw 0-0 with defending World Champions Brazil, and also held Yugoslavia to a 1-1 score-line. Sadly the Scots missed out on the second round on goal difference.

ARGENTINA 1978

THE SCOTS ARRIVED in Argentina full of expectation, but it ended in disappointment. They suffered a shock 3-1 defeat in the first game of the tournament, against Peru, and winger Willie Johnston was sent home in disgrace after failing a drugs test. Further humiliation came when Iran held the Scots to a 1-1 draw. This meant that they needed to beat Holland by three clear goals to progress through to the second round. For a while it looked as though this might become a reality, but their 3-2 win, including one of the great World Cup goals from Archie Gemmill, was not enough.

Archie Gemmill scores for Scotland against Holland, 1978.

SPAIN 1982

SCOTLAND MISSED OUT on the second phase on goal difference for the third World Cup running. They enjoyed their most convincing World Cup win with a 5-2 success over New Zealand in their first match, taking the lead against Brazil before losing 4-1. They went on to draw 2-2 with an impressive Russian side, but it was the goals conceded against Brazil which had the Scots flying home early.

Memorable Moments: Northern Ireland

Northern Ireland have only reached the World Cup finals on three occasions but have twice come up with surprises for some of the fancied sides.

SWEDEN 1958

IRELAND WON their first ever World Cup match, beating Czechoslovakia 1-0. They were outclassed 3-1 by Argentina in their next game but held West Germany to a 2-2 draw. They reached the play-off for the second phase against Czechoslovakia, and defying all odds, reached the last eight courtesy of a 2-1 victory. They crashed 4-0 to France in the quarter finals.

SPAIN 1982

BILLY BINGHAM'S SIDE produced an heroic display to reach the second phase after beating the hosts Spain to finish top of their first round group. They began with a goalless draw against the skilful Yugoslavians before being held to a 1-1 draw by Honduras. They stunned the hosts with a 1-0 victory, taking them into the second round where they drew 2-2 with Austria before falling 4-1 to France.

Memorable Moments: Wales

Wales has made only one appearance in the finals and on this occasion caused a major surprise by qualifying for the quarter-finals.

SWEDEN 1958

THE GREAT John Charles led Wales to three successive draws in their opening group games. The Welsh drew 1-1 with Hungary, held Mexico to the same score-line and then went on to hold the hosts, Sweden, to a goalless draw. Wales triumphed 2-1 in the first round play-off against Hungary but went out of the competition in the quarter-final at the hands of eventual champions Brazil.

Left: the World Cup trophy. Above: Wales vs. Brazil, World Cup 1958.

GREAT PLAYERS, TEAMS AND MANAGERS

Player Profiles

Throughout football history, debate has raged over which players were the best. Changes in fitness levels, technique and tactics make it difficult to compare players from one generation to the next, yet there remains a select band of players whose talents stand the test of time.

GORDON BANKS, ENGLAND

BANKS TOOK GOALKEEPING into the modern age with his attention to fitness and angles, and is remembered for one of the finest saves ever seen. He started his career with Chesterfield in 1958, but moved to First-Division Leicester City, where he made his name before joining Stoke City. He played for England 73 times and once kept clean sheets in seven successive internationals. He was in goal when England won the 1966 World Cup, but his most spectacular moment was in 1970 in Guadalajara – a remarkable leap across his goal to force a fierce close-range Pele header over the bar from an impossible angle. His career was cut short in 1972 when he lost an eye in a car crash:

FRANZ BECKENBAUER,
WEST GERMANY

BECKENBAUER WAS DUBBED the 'Kaiser' due to the commanding presence he brought to a football pitch during the 1960s and 1970s. A midfielder turned defender, he made 103 appearances for his country, during which time he captained the side to victory in the World Cup Final of 1974 against Holland.

Beckenbauer perfected the new role of 'sweeper' in the great German side of the early 1970s. Sitting behind the rest of his defence, he would clear up any danger from the opposition and often turn defence into attack with one pinpoint pass. After hanging up his boots, he was appointed national manager and completed a unique double by steering the West Germans to World Cup glory when they beat Argentina 1-0 in Rome in 1990.

GEORGE BEST, NORTHERN IRELAND

WHEN IT COMES to pure skill and the ability to thrill, George Best is almost without equal. Best was plucked from the obscurity of Belfast and catapulted to fame with Matt Busby's Manchester United. During a golden spell with United in the late 1960s, Best lived up to his name. He won two League Championship medals, scored as Manchester United won the European Cup and was named European Footballer of the Year in 1968. Sadly his liking for the high life – he was dubbed the 'Fifth Beatle' – was his downfall. He failed to cope with his superstar status and the football world was the poorer for his early departure from the game.

BOBBY CHARLTON, ENGLAND

ONE OF THE FEW footballers whose name means as much to those in foreign parts as it does to his home nation. Bobby Charlton survived the 1958 Munich air crash which claimed the lives of so many of his Manchester United team-mates, and went on to inspire his club and country at home and abroad. Playing as a deep-lying centre-forward, Charlton packed a ferocious shot with either foot, which produced some spectacular goals. He was at the heart of England's 1966 World Cup triumph and scored twice as Manchester United won the European Cup in 1968. He won a record 106 caps for his country before finally retiring in 1975. He has since developed a world-wide network of soccer coaching schools for youngsters and is a director at his former club. He was knighted in 1994.

JOHANN CRUYFF, HOLLAND

CRUYFF BROUGHT new meaning to the phrase 'Dutch Master' as he formed the spearhead of the great Holland side of the early 1970s. He joined Ajax aged just 12, made his debut at 17 and scored during his first appearance for his country two years later. Cruyff perfected a new turn which bamboozled some of the world's best defenders and now bears his name. He was named European Footballer of the Year three times running in the early 1970s and became the world's most expensive footballer when he left Ajax for Barcelona in 1973 for a £922,000 transfer. Cruyff won three European Cups during his playing career and after retiring, began a highly successful coaching career which saw him take Ajax to the European Cup-Winners' Cup and Barcelona to European Cup glory.

ALFREDO DI STEFANO, ARGENTINA

MANY FOOTBALL JUDGES place the brilliant Argentinian at the very peak of the all-time list. Di Stefano's amazing pace, stamina and organisational abilities put him head and shoulders above others.

Di Stefano began his career with Argentina's Los Cardales, and moved to the River Plate club before arriving at Spanish giants Real Madrid via a four-year spell in Colombia. It was

with Real Madrid that di Stefano established himself as a world star. Showing a unique ability to defend, create and score goals, he led the brilliant Spaniards to five straight European Cup triumphs – Di Stefano scored in each final. He survived being kidnapped by guerrillas during a Real Madrid tour of Venezuela in 1963 and finally retired from playing in 1965.

DUNCAN EDWARDS, ENGLAND

THE MUNICH AIR crash of 1958 tragically claimed Duncan Edwards as one of its victims, aged just 21. By that time he was already England's youngest twentieth-century international – capped aged just 18 years and 183 days, and had represented his country 18 times in under three years. A powerfully built centre-half, Edwards possessed a delicate touch on the ball and a great goal-scoring ability. After making his League debut at the age of 16, he became captain of Manchester United's famous 'Busby Babes' and would surely have led his country had it not been for the Munich disaster. Edwards survived for 15 days after the crash, but eventually lost his brave fight for life. Just how much Edwards could have achieved will never

be known, but team-mate Bobby Charlton is in no doubt, describing his colleague as 'the greatest of them all'.

EUSEBIO DA SILVA FERREIRA, PORTUGAL

EUSEBIO WAS DUBBED the 'Black Panther' due to his predatory goal-scoring instincts which took him to international fame with Benfica and Portugal. Although he made his name in Portugal, he was actually born in 1942 in Mozambique, coming to Portugal as a result of its links with Mozambique where the

likes of Benfica and Sporting Lisbon supported junior teams. He was on Sporting Lisbon's books but Benfica managed to hijack their rivals and in 13 goal-filled seasons he helped them win the League seven times. He was European Footballer of the Year in 1965, top scorer in the 1966 World Cup with nine goals and scored a remarkable 38 goals in 46 internationals for his adopted country. His sportsmanship endeared him to fans around the world and the Portuguese film industry made a film about his life – *Sua Majestade o Rei* ('His Majesty the King').

GARRINCHA, BRAZIL

GARRINCHA OVERCAME THE EFFECTS of poverty and a childhood illness which left his legs twisted, to become one of the great figures of the 1960s. Doctors who carried out surgery on his legs feared he would struggle to walk properly in later life. Garrincha defied them becoming a fast-raiding right winger with an abundance of skill. He was the star of the winning Brazilian World Cup team of 1962 but his taste for practical jokes often saw him fall foul of coaches. After hanging up his boots, Garrincha's life lost direction and he eventually died from alcoholic poisoning.

RUUD GULLIT, HOLLAND

THE DUTCHMAN WITH the flowing dreadlocks was without equal in Europe in the late 1980s and early 1990s. After starting his career as a sweeper with Haarlem in Holland,

he was converted into a lethal striker with PSV Eindhoven, who sold him to AC Milan in 1987 for a then world-record fee of £6.5 million. Blessed with a powerful combination of pace, skill and strength, he captained Holland to the European Championship the following year and enjoyed European-Cup glory with Milan. He moved to Chelsea in 1995 and a year later was appointed player-coach. They won the FA Cup in his first season, but Gullit left the club the following year and was later appointed manager of Newcastle United.

DIEGO MARADONA, ARGENTINA

MARADONA'S SKILL AND STRENGTH took him to the peak of the world game throughout the 1980s and early 1990s. His volatile temperament and off-pitch drug problems often undermined a talent which has rarely been equalled. His ability was obvious from an early age and he made his League debut for Argentinos Juniors aged just 15. He was selected four months later, aged 16, to represent Argentina – the start of a breath-taking international career. The 1986 World Cup in Mexico

was Maradona's finest period. Despite his 'hand of God' goal against England, he was in unstoppable form and was named player of the tournament. He was banned from the game in 1991 for 15 months after a drugs test found traces of cocaine in his body. He was in more trouble again in 1994 after another positive dope test and his playing career finally staggered to a close in 1997.

STANLEY MATTHEWS, ENGLAND

THE 'WIZARD OF DRIBBLE', Stanley Matthews was the king of the wing over three remarkable decades. Born in Stoke-on-Trent in 1915, he joined his home-town club at the age of 17 and was capped by England two years later. Supporters flocked to see him wherever he played, desperate to catch a glimpse of the famous swerve of the hips which confused and embarrassed full-backs around the world. He moved on to Blackpool where, in the 1953 FA Cup Final, he inspired his team to a 4-3 win against Bolton Wanderers after coming back from 3-1 down. Matthews made the last of 54 England appearances aged 42 – the country's oldest international. He hung up his boots at the age of 50, having never been booked. Regarded as football's 'First Gentleman', he was knighted in 1965.

BOBBY MOORE, ENGLAND

ASSURED OF IMMORTALITY in England after leading his nation to World Cup glory in 1966, Moore won a record 108 caps for his country. He was captain a record 90 times. His positional sense was unequalled, his passing ability was legendary and he was rightly regarded as the best defender of his generation. Moore joined West Ham aged 17 in 1958, making his international debut four years later. He remained at Upton Park for 15 years, winning the FA Cup and European Cup-Winners' Cup and being named Footballer of the Year in 1964. He later steered Fulham to their first-ever FA Cup Final, and a brief managerial spell after hanging up his boots ended in failure, after which he left the game. He subsequently developed cancer, and died aged 51 in 1993.

PELE, BRAZIL

EDSON ARANTES DO NASCIMENTO, or 'Pele', is at the top of any all-time list of greats. During a glittering career Pele's unique blend of skill, speed and strength made him the most prolific goalscorer ever. After being spotted playing for his local club Bauru at the age of 15, he spent most of his career with Brazil's top club Santos. In a remarkable 18-year spell he scored a world-record 1,217 goals in 1,254 matches. He became the

youngest World Cup winner in 1958 aged 17, winning a second winners' medal in 1970 at his peak. He left the world stage in 1974 but was lured out of retirement to play for the New York Cosmos as football tried to gain a stronger hold in the USA. He finally quit in 1977, receiving FIFA's Gold Medal Award for outstanding service to the game in 1982. He has since embarked on a political career, which saw his appointment as Brazil's Minister for Sport.

MICHEL PLATINI, FRANCE

THIS GIFTED MIDFIELDER was one of the giants of the game in the early 1980s. A creative player with a deadly eye for goals from free-kicks, Platini inspired France to fourth place at the 1982 World Cup. After starting his career with Nancy Lorraine, he made his name with Saint-Etienne before joining Juventus after his World Cup heroics. He was the top scorer in the notoriously defensive Italian League three years running and scored the penalty which gave Juventus their first European Cup success in 1985. Platini worked as a broadcaster and businessman after leaving the game but

was briefly lured back to manage his country for the 1992 European Championship. When the team failed to live up to expectations he quit and later became one of the key figures in France's staging of the 1998 World Cup.

FERENC PUSKAS, HUNGARY AND SPAIN

PUSKAS WAS THE captain of the 'Magic Magyars' – the Hungarian team which took European football to a new level in the 1950s. He was a lethal striker and made his debut for Kispest aged 16 in 1943. He was selected for the national side within two years and captained Hungary in their 1952 Olympic Games victory. He was instrumental in their famous 6-3 triumph over England in 1953, when they were the first foreign side to win at Wembley. During a four year spell, Puskas and Hungary remained unbeaten. Puskas scored an amazing 83 goals in 84 internationals before fleeing to Spain to escape the 1956 uprising. He joined Real Madrid and went on to represent his adopted country at the 1962 World Cup Finals. He retired in 1966 and embarked on a successful business career which he interrupted for brief coaching spells, the last when he temporarily took over as manager of Hungary in 1993.

ROBERTO RIVELINO, BRAZIL

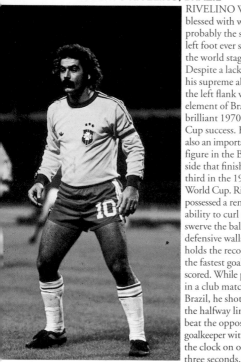

RIVELINO WAS blessed with what was probably the sweetest left foot ever seen on the world stage. Despite a lack of pace, his supreme ability on the left flank was a key element of Brazil's brilliant 1970 World Cup success. He was also an important figure in the Brazilian side that finished third in the 1974 World Cup. Rivelino possessed a remarkable ability to curl and swerve the ball round defensive walls and holds the record for the fastest goal ever scored. While playing in a club match in Brazil, he shot from the halfway line to beat the opposing goalkeeper with the clock on only three seconds.

PETER SHILTON, ENGLAND

WITH 125 INTERNATIONAL appearances to his name, Peter Shilton is England's most capped player. He made his first international appearance at the age of 20 and his last in the 1990 World Cup Finals aged 40. After starting his career as understudy to Gordon Banks at Leicester City, Shilton, a self-confessed perfectionist, turned the art of goalkeeping into something of a science. He conceded only 80 international goals during his long England career and was superb in the late 1970s when Nottingham Forest won the European Cup. Shilton went on to make a record 1,005 Football League appearances and had a brief but unhappy spell in management with Plymouth Argyle.

LEV YASHIN, RUSSIA

WHEN LEV Yashin died aged 61 in 1990, the official Soviet news agency, Tass, described him as 'the most famous Soviet sportsman ever'. Bearing in mind the sporting greats produced by that giant state, it gives an idea of the ability of a player regarded by many as the best-ever goalkeeper. Yashin broke into the great Moscow Dynamo side in 1953 and was called up to the national team a year later. He went on to make a then Soviet record of 78 international appearances and in 1963 became the only goalkeeper ever to be named European Footballer of the Year. He appeared in three World Cups and is reputed to have saved 150 penalties in his career, which ended in 1970. After hanging up his gloves he became head of the Ministry of Sport's football department and was later vice-president of the country's football association. In 1968 he was awarded the supreme Soviet honour of the Order of Lenin.

DINO ZOFF, ITALY

DINO ZOFF is Italy's most capped international with 112 appearances to his credit. His 15-year international career included a spell in 1973 and 1974 which saw Zoff go unbeaten by an opposing forward for 1,143 minutes, spanning 13 international matches. He started his career with Udinese before moving on to Mantova and Napoli, but it was with Juventus that Zoff really made his name. He helped them win League, Cup and European Cup-Winners' Cup honours and, following his retirement, later returned to the club as coach and steered them to the 1990 UEFA Cup. He subsequently moved to Lazio as coach, going on to become club president.

Team Profiles

Like fine wine, great football teams are not made overnight. They evolve gradually with subtle changes being made over a number of years. However, each decade since the Second World War has produced teams which have clearly been a step ahead of the rest.

HUNGARY, 1950s

THE 'MAGIC MAGYARS' led by Ferenc Puskas took football to a new plane in the 1950s. Their 6-3 victory over England at Wembley in 1953 was the first time a foreign team had triumphed at what is regarded as the home of soccer. They brought a whole new tactical approach to the game and were rated at the time as the best side ever thanks to a run of just one international defeat in five years. In that golden period their prolific forwards scored 173 goals, yet they failed to land the World Cup when they lost to West Germany 3-2 in the 1954 Final in Switzerland.

REAL MADRID, 1956–60

THE SPANISH GIANTS were without equal in a remarkable spell which saw them win the European Cup five years running. Centre-forward Alfredo Di Stefano, Hungary's Ferenc Puskas, Jose Santamaria of Uruguay and Brazil's Didi were all attracted to the club which became an irresistible force. An extraordinary 7-3 victory over German champions Eintracht Frankfurt in the 1960 European Cup Final is still hailed by many as the greatest match ever. Puskas scored four and Di Stefano three.

Real Madrid before their victory over Eintracht Frankfurt in 1960.

MANCHESTER UNITED, 1956–58

ENGLISH LEAGUE CHAMPIONS in 1956 and 1957, experts are agreed that this side had the potential to be the most successful ever. With the incomparable Duncan Edwards in defence, the prolific Tommy Taylor in attack and a host of internationals throughout the side, they were poised to sweep all before them. They reached the semi-final of the European Cup in 1957 and were set for another long run the following season when tragedy struck on Thursday, 6 February 1958. Returning from a European Cup match in Yugoslavia, their plane crashed on take-off from Munich Airport. Eight players – Edwards, Taylor, Roger Byrne, Geoff Bent, Eddie Colman, Mark Jones, Bill Whelan and David Pegg, died along with 15 other passengers. Some survived, including manager Matt Busby and Bobby Charlton, but the football world was left mourning a great side and wondering what might have been.

Above: Manchester United, English League Chgampions, 1957.

CELTIC, 1967

CELTIC HAVE been at the peak of the Scottish game ever since they were founded in 1888. In 1967 they produced a side which was at the summit of the game across Europe. An extraordinary season saw them win every competition for which they entered. The Scottish League Cup, FA Cup and League titles all ended up at Parkhead, before the crowning glory arrived in the form of the European Cup. Managed by former player Jock Stein, the Scots beat Internazionale 2-1 in the final in Lisbon. It was the first time a British club had won Europe's biggest prize and the first time any team had completed a clean sweep of trophies. To get there they had scored 200 goals in 64 matches.

The unbeatable team from Celtic in 1967.

BRAZIL, 1970

BRAZIL HAVE WON the World Cup a record four times, but
the side which lifted the trophy in Mexico in 1970 is regarded
as the best of the lot. While not being blessed with the
strongest defence, their attacking flair has rarely been equalled.
With the great Pele at his peak, the Brazilians scored 19 goals
in the six matches. Winger Jairzinho scored in every game,
while the brilliance of Rivelino and Gerson in midfield had
oppositions chasing shadows. Showing extraordinary skill and
invention, they thrashed a notoriously defence-minded Italy
4-1 in the most one-sided final on record.

World Cup team from Brazil, 1970.

AJAX, 1971–73

AT THE START of the 1970s, the Dutch club won the European Cup three years running with the great Johann Cruyff at the heart of their success. The key to their dominance was the concept of 'total football' which saw highly skilled players throw off the restrictions of playing in just one position. Defenders would appear in attack and vice-versa as the Dutch displayed an individual and collective versatility never seen before. Ajax formed the nucleus of the Dutch national side which went so close to winning the 1974 World Cup.

Ajax, European Cup winners, 1973.

BAYERN MUNICH, 1974–76

BAYERN MUNICH have dominated German football across the decades but they pulled off a hat-trick of European Cup victories in 1974, 1975 and 1976. Inspired by skipper Franz Beckenbauer and with fellow internationals Sepp Maier in goal and Gerd Muller up front, the Germans were then without equal in European club football. In 1976 they also won the World Club Cup, a one-off game between the champions of Europe and South America.

NOTTINGHAM FOREST, 1977–80

NOTTINGHAM Forest leaped from the obscurity of the English Second Division to a double European Cup triumph in four short seasons. They won the 1977–78 Championship in their first season after returning to the First Division, and set a League record when they went 42 matches without defeat. They took the European Cup the following season by beating Swedish club Malmo 1-0, and successfully defended the trophy with a 1-0 success over Hamburg the following year.

England striker Trevor Francis apart, they were a team without any true stars, but had a perfect blend of skill and courage, and the inspirational management of the mercurial Brian Clough provided the platform for success.

Bayern Munich with the European Cup, 1975.

LIVERPOOL, 1984

OF ALL THE CLUBS mentioned here, Liverpool get the longevity award. During an unprecedented period of domestic and European dominance, the Anfield side won the League title 10 times in 15 trophy-laden seasons. Yet it was the 1984 side which was the most successful. During a remarkable campaign in manager Joe Fagan's first season in charge, they won the Championship for the third year running, the League Cup (or the Milk Cup as it was then called) for the fourth year in succession, and topped it all off by lifting the European Cup. The team was perfectly balanced: Kenny Dalglish and Ian Rush got the goals, Graeme Souness ran the show in midfield and Mark Lawrenson and Alan Hansen proved to be impeccable in defence.

MANCHESTER UNITED, 1998–99

ON THE 26 MAY 1999 Manchester achieved every club's dream: the Treble. They took the League after beating Tottenham Hotspur in the final match of the season. The FA Cup was clinched as they beat Newcastle 2–0 – Teddy Sheringham coming off the bench to score – making them the first team ever to win the double three times. Facing Bayern Munich in the European Championship, the German team scored in the first few minutes of the game and looked to be certain winners. As the match clicked into injury time, some fans left, unable to watch this great team lose. However, the game was to provide one of the greatest turnarounds in soccer history as, once again, substitute Sheringham put the ball in the back of the net in the 90th minute. Within seconds Ole

Gunnar Solskjaer sealed the deal for the Treble with United's second goal. 31 years after Best and Charlton won the European Cup, on what would have been Sir Matt Busby's 90th birthday, in Schmeichel's last game for the club (and on the night he captained his team), Manchester United made history.

A jubilant Manchester United after winning the match that earned them the Treble.

Manager Profiles

The success or failure of a club or national side often depends on its manager; the skills employed in training, tactics and morale are essential in creating a tight team. Managers have a tough job, but some of the best have led their sides to the very top.

SIR MATT BUSBY

BUSBY CREATED three trophy-winning sides during nearly 30 years at the helm of Manchester United. A Scottish international wing-half who played for Liverpool and Manchester City in the 1930s, he took over at Old Trafford in 1945. Within three years he led the club to FA Cup Final victory, but it was the young team he created in the 1950s which made his name. Dubbed the 'Busby Babes' due to the young players in the side, Busby's clever tactics took them to successive League titles in 1956 and 1957. That team was tragically decimated in the 1958 Munich air crash. Busby himself almost lost his life but thankfully survived to create another great side which included Bobby Charlton, George Best and Denis Law. They won the League Championship in 1967, becoming the first English club to win the European Cup the following season.

HERBERT CHAPMAN

CHAPMAN WAS the first to bring 'professionalism' to the art of football management. He played for Tottenham early in the 1900s without rising to any great heights but had a unique ability to spot talent and bring the best out of players. He joined Huddersfield Town in 1921 when the club had little money, poor crowds and an inferior side. Four years later they won the first of a hat-trick of Championship titles. Having achieved the seemingly impossible, Chapman repeated the feat after joining Arsenal in 1925. They had just avoided relegation when he arrived but within a year finished runners-up to Huddersfield.

After introducing a revolutionary new tactical formation

they won the FA Cup in 1930 and enjoyed three Championship victories in 1933, 1934, and 1935. Chapman suggested floodlit football 20 years before it arrived, tried out numbered shirts five years before they were approved and advocated using white footballs and all-weather pitches. He also demanded decent facilities for spectators. Such was his effect on Arsenal that his bust greets visitors to their Highbury stadium.

BRIAN CLOUGH

IN THE 1970s Clough brought Championship success to two clubs which had previously never dreamed of reaching such dizzy heights. A prolific goal-scorer – he scored 251 goals in 275 league games for Middlesbrough and Sunderland – Clough retired due to injury and plunged into management with Fourth Division Hartlepool. With his assistant Peter Taylor, he joined struggling Second Division Derby County in 1967. His unique man-management skills brought the best out of previously average players and Derby won the League title for the first time in 1972. They reached the semi-final of the European Cup the following season, before Clough took over at Second Division Nottingham Forest in 1975, following a season with Brighton and just 44 days at Leeds United. After winning promotion in 1977, Forest won the League Championship and League Cup the following year before winning the European Cup in consecutive seasons.

STAN CULLIS

CULLIS LED Wolverhampton Wanderers to three League Championships in 1954, 1958 and 1959. He had been a powerful centre-half with Wolves and England and brought a military-like discipline to his sides. He was the first to employ the long-ball tactic and critics described the style as 'kick and rush'. Although the system was not pretty to watch, it was effective. When they pulled off two historic friendly victories over Russian champions Moscow Spartak and Hungary's powerful Honved side, Cullis described the team as 'champions of the world'. His remark led to the birth of the European Cup.

KENNY DALGLISH

DALGLISH HAS led different clubs to the English Championship. After a remarkable playing career with Celtic, Liverpool and Scotland, he became player-manager at Anfield in 1985, leading Liverpool to the League and FA Cup double in his first season. That first year was tarnished by the Heysel Stadium tragedy that occurred in the 1984–85 season, in which 39 football fans died. After this, Dalglish led Liverpool to two further title wins, although he was again thrown into the centre of tragedy when 95 Liverpool fans died in the Hillsborough disaster in 1989. Dalglish resigned suddenly in 1991, but later returned to management with Second Division Blackburn and in 1995 he took them to their first League title. He moved to Newcastle in 1997 and took the club to the 1999 FA Cup Final, where they lost to Manchester United.

SIR ALEX FERGUSON

FERGUSON HAS taken Manchester United back to the top of the English game after almost 30 years. The Scot initially enjoyed success with Aberdeen, where he took charge in 1978. In eight seasons he led Aberdeen to three Scottish titles, four Scottish FA Cups, the Scottish League Cup and the 1983 European Cup Winners' Cup. His arrival at Old Trafford in 1986 did not produce results overnight. His team flattered to deceive and while the fans grew restless, the board kept patient and in 1990 Ferguson's United won the FA Cup. The European Cup-Winners' Cup and League Cup followed, but it was not until 1993 that the much-awaited prize of the League Championship was finally secured. The following season United clinched the League and FA Cup double, a feat they repeated two seasons later, thus becoming the first side to do the double twice. In 1999 they became the first team to win the Treble – and Ferguson received a knighthood.

BOB PAISLEY

WHEN IT COMES to winning trophies Bob Paisley is the most successful manager in English football history. During nine years in charge at Liverpool between 1974 and 1983,

Paisley took the team to 20 trophies, including six League titles, three European Cups, three League Cups and one European Cup-Winners' Cup. As a player, trainer and assistant manager at Liverpool, Paisley was perfectly placed to take over when his predecessor Bill Shankly stepped down. Despite his relaxed image, he displayed a ruthless streak and timed his transfer market dealings to perfection. The loss of England captain Kevin Keegan was barely noticed as Kenny Dalglish was brought in as the perfect replacement.

SIR ALF RAMSEY

SIR ALF will always be remembered by English football fans as the man who led the nation to their only World Cup success, in 1966. An England international full-back, Ramsey cut his managerial teeth at Ipswich. He took the Suffolk side to an unlikely Championship victory in 1962 and became England's first full-time manager in 1963. He boldly predicted the side would win the World Cup and his determination and tactical awareness duly took England to an unparalleled triumph. In an era when wingers were seen as the best route to victory, Ramsey's England played the final matches without any. His new 4-4-2 formation with four defenders, four midfielders and two attackers became the accepted way to play for almost 20 years. He was knighted in honour of this victory and went on to become England's longest serving manager of the modern era before being dismissed when they failed to reach the 1974 World Cup finals. He died in 1999, still the hero of a nation.

BILL SHANKLY

SHANKLY IS RESPONSIBLE for establishing Liverpool as a major force in English soccer. When the former Scottish international half-back arrived at Anfield in 1959, they were struggling in the Second Division. When he finally retired from the game in 1974, the man who once said that football

was more important than life or death had created a dynasty which is still paying dividends today. Preaching a simple 'pass and move' philosophy, Shankly took Liverpool into the First Division in 1962 and they landed the League Championship two seasons later. Two more titles and the FA Cup followed, but it was his uncanny ability to spot young talent that set Shankly apart. Players like Ray Clemence and Kevin Keegan were signed from lower League sides and nurtured in the Anfield reserves before exploding on to the first-team scene.

JOCK STEIN

A FORMER CELTIC player, Stein presided over the most successful period in the Parkhead club's illustrious history. After taking over in 1965, he took Celtic to ten League titles, seven FA Cups, six League Cups and the 1967 European Cup. In that 1966–67 season Stein's side won every competition they entered – the Scottish League title, Scottish FA Cup, the League Cup, as well as the European Cup. He was at the helm as Celtic romped to a record nine successive League Championships, including back to back League and Cup doubles in 1971 and 1972. Stein retired in 1977 but made a brief comeback with Leeds United before being appointed Scotland manager in 1978. He died aged just 62, when he suffered a heart attack on the touchline as Scotland drew with Wales in a World Cup qualifying game in 1985.

LAWS OF THE GAME

First Laws

The first laws of football were drawn up at Cambridge University in 1848 by Messrs H. de Winton and J. C. Thring. They wanted to rationalise the way the game was played in the nation's public schools and universities.

IT TOOK nearly eight hours for the meeting to settle on 10 rules which were to be adopted from then on. No copy of those original rules exist today. The earliest set, thought to be almost identical to the first, dates back to 1862. They were also issued by Mr Thring for what he described as 'The Simplest Game'. They are reproduced on the facing page.

Football match in 1878.

RULES FOR THE SIMPLEST GAME
Issued by J.C. Thring, 1862

1   A goal is scored whenever the ball is forced through the goal and under the bar, except it be thrown by hand.

2   Hands may be used only to stop a ball and place it on the ground before the feet.

3   Kicks must be aimed only at the ball.

4   A player may not kick the ball whilst in the air

5   No tripping up or heel kicking allowed.

6   Whenever a ball is kicked beyond the side flags, it must be returned by the player who kicked it, from the spot it passed the flag-line, in a straight line towards the middle of the ground.

7   When a ball is kicked behind the line of goal, it shall be kicked off from that line by one of the side whose goal it is.

8   No player may stand within six paces of the kicker when he is kicking off.

9   A player is 'out of play' immediately he is in front of the ball and must return behind the ball as soon as possible. If the ball is kicked by his own side past a player, he may not touch or kick it, or advance, until one of the other side has first kicked it, or one of his own side has been able to kick it on a level with, or in front of him.

10   No charging allowed when a player is 'out of play'; that is, immediately the ball is behind him.

Rule Milestones

The purpose of forming the Football Association (FA) in 1863 was to establish a uniform set of laws by which all clubs and schools could play the game. Some elements of the Cambridge Rules were incorporated.

The Football Association shield.

SINCE THE ADOPTION of these laws, finally agreed after five FA meetings, football has embarked on a constant search to sharpen up the game's regulations. There is an annual review by FIFA, and eight votes are cast on any proposed law change – four from England, Scotland, Wales and Northern Ireland and four from FIFA. Three-quarters have to be in favour for a law change to be adopted. Highlighted below are some of the major law changes over the decades.

1872	Size of ball fixed
1875	Crossbar replaces tape
1882	Two-handed throw-in introduced
1891	Goal nets and penalties introduced
1891	Referees and linesmen replace umpire and referees
1898	Promotion and relegation begins
1905	Goalkeeper must stay on line at penalties
1924	Goal can be scored direct from a corner
1925	Offside rule changed. Two players rather than three needed between attacker and goal
1951	White ball introduced
1965	Substitutes allowed for injured players
1981	Three points for a win
1990	Offside rule changed again. Attacker level with defender is no longer offside
1990	'Professional' foul made sending-off offence

Simple Guide to the Laws of the Game

OBJECT OF THE GAME

In many respects football is the simplest of games. The object is to propel the ball by any part of the body other than the hand or arms into the opponent's goal. The whole of the ball must pass over the opponent's goal-line for a goal to be scored. The winner is the team which has achieved this more times than the opposition by the end of the match.

THE PITCH

UNDER LAW ONE the 'field of play' must measure between 90 m (100 yd) and 120 m (130 yd) and be 45 m (50 yd) to 90 m (100 yd) wide. It must always be rectangular, with the length exceeding the width.

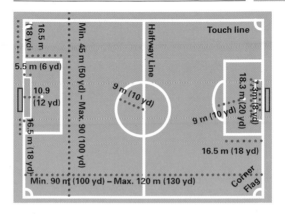

16.5 m (18 yd)

Min. 45 m (50 yd) – Max. 90 (100 yd)

5.5 m (6 yd)

Halfway Line

Touch line

10.9 (12 yd)

9 m (10 yd)

18.3 m (20 yd)

7.3 m (8 yd)

16.5 m (18 yd)

9 m (10 yd)

16.5 m (18 yd)

Min. 90 m (100 yd) – Max. 120 m (130 yd)

Corner Flag

LINES ON THE PITCH

TOUCHLINES ARE LINES drawn down the side of the pitch, while those across the pitch at each end are goal-lines. The halfway line is drawn at a point half-way between the two goal-lines. A centre spot from where play starts and re-starts after a goal or half-time is drawn in the middle, around which is drawn a circle with a 9.15 m (10 yd) radius. The lines are 12 cm (5 in) wide and are in play.

Each corner of the field must have a corner flag with a minimum height of 1.5 m (5 ft). A quadrant with a 1 m (1 yd) radius is drawn at each corner.

Left: Ian Rush scores Liverpool's third goal in the 1986 FA Cup Final.

GOAL POSTS

AT EACH END of the field is a goal consisting of two uprights placed 7.32 m (8 yd) apart from the inside of each post. These are joined at the top by a crossbar 2.44 m (8 ft) in height. The uprights and crossbars should not exceed 12 cm (5 in) in width.

GOAL AREA

THIS IS CREATED at each end. Two lines are drawn at right angles to the goal-line 5.5 m (6 yd) from each post. They reach into the field of play for 5.5 m (6 yd) where they are joined by a line parallel to the goal-line. This defines the goal area which is then enclosed in the larger penalty area. This is created by drawing two lines at right angles to the goal-line 16.5 m (18 yd) from each goal post and extending into the field of play by 16.5 m (18 yd). These are joined by a line of 40.3 m (44 yd) running parallel to the goal-line.

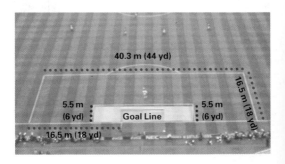

40.3 m (44 yd)

16.5 m (18 yd)

5.5 m (6 yd)   Goal Line   5.5 m (6 yd)

16.5 m (18 yd)

PENALTY MARK

THIS IS DRAWN 11 m (12 yd) from the goal-line, in line with the middle of the goal. To guarantee all players apart from the penalty taker are 9.15 m (10 yd) from the ball at a penalty, an arc with a 9.15 m (10 yd) radius is drawn 9.15 m (10 yd) from the penalty mark itself.

No other lines are officially allowed on the pitch. Goal-keepers who mark the 5.5 m (6 yd) area by scraping their boots on the ground to help them judge angles are technically infringing the laws.

Action in the goalmouth: Yeovil vs. Aldershot, 1955.

The Team and Players

Two teams of 11 players are required to play a football game, although a side can now involve up to **14** players, including three substitutes. Depending on the rules of individual competitions, that number can be reduced, but the International Board has stated that no game can be valid if there are fewer than seven players in either team taking part.

THE TEAM must include a goalkeeper who wears clothing which distinguishes from his team-mates. Any player can change with the goalkeeper at any time during a stoppage in play, as long as the referee is informed. If a goalkeeper is sent off for foul play, a substitute goalkeeper can be used so long as an outfield player leaves the pitch to reduce the side to 10 players.

If a player is sent off before the match starts, which can happen, a named substitute can be used. This is also the case if a team starts a game with fewer than 11 men. Late arrivals, provided they have been put down as named substitutes, can join the play.

Michael Rumminigge of Borussia Dortmund.

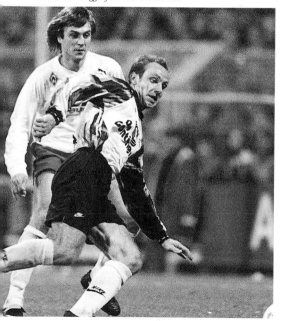

Equipment

The basic equipment required by all players consists of a jersey or shirt, shorts, socks, shin guards and footwear. Cycling shorts or thermopants have been allowed in recent years, providing they are predominantly the same colour as the player's shorts.

FOOTWEAR

THE LAW DOES not detail precisely what sort of footwear is appropriate although it must not present a danger. Most players wear boots with studs or bars in them. Studs are usually made of nylon, aluminium, rubber or leather for wet conditions, while moulded rubber studs are normally more suitable for hard pitches. In northern Europe, where players

Most football boots have studs to help grip the pitch.

have to perform on frozen pitches a special 'ice' stud has been developed. Referees or their assistants will check studs before matches to ensure that they are safe.

OTHER RULES

THE GOALKEEPER must wear distinguishing clothing so he can be differentiated from other players. No player should wear anything which could cause harm to another player. Jewellery should be removed or in the case of rings, taped up. Referees should insist that players wearing jewellery remove the offending item. If the player refuses, they can be stopped from playing.

THE BALL

JUST ABOUT ANY ROUND OBJECT has been used for impromptu games of football, but Law Two of the game stipulates precise measurements and weights for the ball in official games. To fulfil the requirements, it has to be round and must be leather or any other material approved by the International Board. It cannot be more than 70 cm (28 in) or less than 67.5 cm (28 in) in circumference, and must not weigh more than 448 g (16 oz) or less than 390 g (14 oz).

The ball must be round and made of leather.

Duration of a Match

In senior football for those aged 18 and above, matches last for 90 minutes with two equal periods of 45 minutes. These times are reduced according to the age of the players involved. Each half is separated by an interval which should last a minimum of five minutes. In the modern professional game, it is often nearer 15 minutes.

IN SOME COMPETITIONS, extra-time can be played if the teams are level at the end of normal play. In senior matches this extra period lasts 30 minutes and consists of 15-minute halves with sides changing ends at the close of the first period.

The 'golden goal' was first introduced to the World Cup in 1998, which meant that the first side to score during extra-time automatically won the game. Cup games which remain deadlocked are often decided by way of a penalty shootout, although some competitions allow for replayed matches. The referee is the game's time-keeper. Extra-time can be added for stoppages for injuries, cautions or substitutions.

Right: Stuart Pearce, after missing in England's penalty shoot-out against West Germany, World Cup 1990.

The Kick-off

Prior to the match, the two captains meet the referee to toss a coin for the choice of ends. The winning captain's side chooses either to kick off or selects their end of play.

AT THE KICK-OFF, the ball is placed on the centre spot and must be kicked forwards by one of the attackers. All 11 players from each side must start on their own half of the pitch. Opposing players must be at least 9.15 m (10 yd) from the ball. The ball has to be stationary and is in play once it has travelled its full circumference in the opponents' half. The player taking the kick-off is not allowed to play the ball again until it has been touched by another player.

The same procedure is followed every time a goal is scored, or to start the second half when the two teams change ends. The second-half kick-off is done by the opposing side to that which took the first.

Celebrities are sometimes invited to perform the kick-off at charity or showpiece games. In reality this should not count, as the celebrity is not a member of a team and under the laws a second kick-off should be staged.

Bolton and West Ham captains shake hands before kick-off, FA Cup Final 1923.

A Goal

A GOAL IS SCORED if the ball crosses the whole of the
goal-line, providing it was not propelled by a hand or arm.
It must not be thrown or carried and if it strikes the hand or
arm of any player or the referee and is deflected over the line, a
goal should stand.

Martin Peters scores for England in their triumphant 1966 World Cup Final.

Corner-kicks

A CORNER KICK IS AWARDED to the attacking team if the ball is played over the goal-line on either side of the goal by a member of the defending team.

The kick should be taken from within the quadrant at the corner flag and on the side of the goal where the ball crossed the line.

Defenders must remain 9.15 m (10 yd) from the ball, and the player taking the kick must not touch it again until another player has played the ball. The taker is not allowed to remove a corner flag even if it is impeding his route to the ball.

A goal can be scored direct from a corner-kick without anyone else touching the ball.

Stanley Matthews takes a corner, 1943.

Throw-ins

A THROW-IN is awarded when the ball crosses the touchline. Possession goes to the side opposing that of the player who put it out of play. It must be taken from as close to the point where the ball crossed the touchline as possible. If it is not thrown from the right place, it will be ruled a foul throw and possession will go back to the other side.

The ball must be thrown two-handed from behind, and over the head. The thrower's feet must remain on the ground during the throw, on or behind the touchline when the ball is released. Failure to follow this procedure will result in a foul throw.

Goal-kicks

A GOAL-KICK WILL be awarded to the defending side when the ball is played over the goal-line. It is normally, but not compulsorily, taken by the goalkeeper, and can be taken from either side of the goal regardless of which side it went out of play. Opposing players must be outside the penalty area when a goal-kick is taken. The ball is not back in play until it has passed out of the penalty area. Following an alteration to the rules in 1997, a goal can be scored from a goal-kick.

Vinny Jones throws-in for Wales, 1994.

Indirect Free-kicks

These will be awarded when a player commits minor
or technical infringements of the laws of the game or
does anything which the referee rules to be
'unsporting conduct' (previously defined
as 'ungentlemanly').

A GOAL CANNOT be scored from an indirect free-kick
unless the ball is touched by another player before crossing
the goal-line. If an attacker plays the ball into the net and it is
not touched by anyone else, a goal-kick will be awarded.

Defenders must be at least 9.15 m (10 yd) from the ball
when it is kicked.

An indirect free-kick should be taken from the spot where
an infringement occurred.

Indirect free-kicks can be awarded for any of the following types of offences:

- offside (explained in detail on page 155)
- dangerous play
- obstructing an opponent's progress while not attempting to play the ball
- preventing a goalkeeper from releasing the ball from their hands
- playing the ball twice from a corner, free-kick or other re-start before another player has touched it
- unsporting conduct
- goalkeeper taking more than four steps while holding, bouncing or throwing the ball
- goalkeeper holding the ball for more than six seconds
- goalkeeper touching the ball with his hands before it has been touched by another player outside the area
- goalkeeper touching the ball with his or her hands after it has been deliberately kicked back or thrown back (via a throw-in) by a team-mate
- time-wasting tactics

N.B. A referee can play the 'advantage' rule and let the game continue if the side against whom an offence is committed is in possession and would be disadvantaged if the game was stopped.

Indirect free-kicks must be touched by another player before a goal can be scored.

Direct Free-kicks

These are awarded for more serious offences. If any of these 'penal' fouls are committed in the penalty area, a penalty is awarded.

A GOAL CAN be scored from a direct free-kick without another player touching the ball. Defenders again need to be 9.15 m (10 yd) from the ball when it is kicked.

The free-kick is taken from the spot where the offence was committed except when a defending team is awarded a free-kick in their own goal area. It can be taken from any part of the goal area.

The ball must be stationary and players must wait for a signal from the referee to take the kick.

Direct free-kicks will be awarded for the following offences:

- kicking or attempting to kick an opponent
- striking or attempting to strike an opponent
- spitting at an opponent
- tripping or attempting to trip an opponent
- jumping at an opponent
- charging an opponent
- holding
- pushing
- when tackling, making contact with an opponent before the ball
- deliberate handball

Andy Hinchcliffe takes a free-kick in the FA Carling Premiership, 1998.

Penalty Kick

Penalties will be awarded if any of the 'penal' fouls outlined earlier are committed in the penalty area. They can be given by the referee regardless of where the ball is in play at the time the offence is committed.

A GOAL CAN be scored directly from the kick, which is taken from the penalty spot. The only players allowed into the penalty area until the ball is struck are the penalty taker and the opposing goalkeeper.

If any other player from either side encroaches into the area before the ball is kicked, the referee can order the kick to be retaken. The goalkeeper can move about on the goal-line before the kick, but must not move forwards.

Once the kick is taken, the penalty taker cannot touch the ball a second time until it has been touched by another player.

If the defending team infringe any of the penalty rules and the kick is missed, the referee will order it to be retaken. If a goal is scored, it will be allowed. If the penalty taker breaches

Alan Shearer appeals for a penalty, 1995.

any penalty rule, an indirect free-kick is awarded against him or her.

Extra-time must be added at half-time or full-time to allow a penalty kick to be taken or retaken if necessary. The time extension lasts until a goal has been scored, missed or saved.

Offside Law

Offside is without doubt the most controversial law in the game of football, and the source of some of the game's fiercest arguments.

THE OFFSIDE LAW is one of the most difficult for the referee to judge. At its simplest, a player is deemed to be offside if, at the moment the ball is passed, only the goalkeeper is between the opposing player and the goal line.

However, a player is *not* offside if the ball is played to them by an opponent; or if they are in their own half of the field at the time; or the player receives the ball from a goal-kick, corner-kick or throw-in.

A player is not offside if they are behind the ball when it is played, even if there are no defenders between them and the goal.

The biggest problem with the law for officials, players and referees is making the judgement of where the receiving player was at the moment the ball was played and whether the attacker was 'seeking to gain an advantage' at the time.

In recent years, officials have been urged to give any benefit of the doubt to the attacking side.

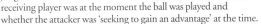

It is often difficult to judge if a player is offside.

Football Punishments

The referee can issue a caution or booking to a player
for any offences deemed serious.

The laws stipulate that a player shall be booked and shown
a yellow card if they:

- persistently infringe the laws
- enter or leave the pitch without permission
- show dissent
- show unsporting conduct, particularly if
  encroaching or kicking the ball
  away at a free-kick

For the most serious offences, a player
can instantly be shown a red card and
sent off. These offences include:

- any player guilty of violent
  conduct
- use of foul or abusive language
- a defender who impedes an
  opponent during a goalscoring
  opportunity
- deliberate handball in the
  penalty area to prevent a
  goalscoring opportunity
- a player previously cautioned
  and persisting in misconduct

Bradford City goalkeeper Gary Walsh gets shown the yellow card.

PLAYING THE GAME

Becoming a Player

Millions of youngsters around the globe have been introduced to the game of football by their parents or pals. Two coats thrown down in a garden, street, beach or backyard are more often than not enough to form a pitch, while everything from tin cans to rolled up balls of paper have been used to get a game going.

HERE IN BRITAIN today, youngsters have more opportunities than ever to play the game in an organised way. It is still the most popular sport in the country's schools, while there are youth teams in almost every town and village.

The Football Association itself runs highly popular 'Soccer Funweeks' for youngsters during school holidays. These are run by qualified coaches and give children aged six and above vital tips on how to become better players.

Football has always been a game of dreams, and youngsters who show early promise will quickly find themselves attending 'Schools of Excellence'. These are special coaching centres run by professional clubs where the potential stars of tomorrow are given special advice and guidance to make the most of their ability.

For those beyond school age, there has never been more on offer to indulge a footballing passion. Thousands of clubs operate up and down the country, be they pub sides turning

Ally McCoist, then of Rangers, with a keen young player.

out for friendly games with rival villages or semi-professional teams run on similar lines to their full-time counterparts in the Football League.

Kit Requirements

Law 4 of the Rules of the Game states: 'the basic compulsory equipment of a player shall consist of a jersey or shirt, shorts, stockings [socks], shinguards and footwear. A player shall not wear anything which is dangerous to another player. The goalkeeper shall wear colours which will distinguish him from the otherplayers and the referee.'

KIT HISTORY

WHEN FOOTBALL became organised in the 1870s, it was very much a game for the 'gentlemen' of the day. As a result their attire was formal in the extreme. In the first international between England and Scotland in 1872, England players wore white jerseys, dark blue caps and white knickerbockers. However as the game spread to the 'masses', the clothing became

simpler – and cheaper – and design changes apart, has remained consistent for the better part of 100 years.

BOOTS

IN THE NINETEENTH century the earliest players nailed studs into their working boots to get a grip on the pitch. By the 1920s they were playing in ankle-length boots. They remained like this until the late 1950s when the shoe-type design of today first appeared. Specially designed soles were also produced to allow screw-in nylon studs to be used.

Today, scientists employed by the major manufacturers are constantly striving to find the most comfortable or 'powerful' boot. The best boots are made out of kangaroo leather with aluminium studs and moulded plastic soles.

Left: by the rules of the game, the goalkeeper must wear clothes that distinguish him from the other players.
Top: shirts from the early days of football.
Bottom: the shoe-type boot was first used in the 1950s.

SHIRTS

THE FIRST FOOTBALL shirts were made out of wool, but this quickly gave way to cotton. At the turn of the century, they had lace-up collars, a style which resurfaced in the late 1990s. Cotton was the mainstay of shirts until the late 1960s when the development of synthetic materials produced an even cheaper and more versatile way of making shirts. Numbered shirts were not compulsory before 1939. Until 1982, the rules stated that goalkeepers could only wear green, yellow or white shirts.

Modern shirts are made from synthetic materials.

SHINPADS

THE FIRST SHINPADS were worn by Sam Weller Widdowson of Nottingham Forest and England in 1874. They were originally worn outside the socks and despite the risk of injury, many players have been reluctant to wear them because they considered them a hindrance to running. They were made compulsory in 1991 by FIFA following medical advice regarding lower leg injuries. Rolled-up newspapers, paperback books or magazines have all been used, but shinpads are now predominantly made of polyurethane.

BALL

HISTORY BOOKS show pigs' bladders were among the earliest objects to be employed as a ball. From the early twentieth century, the ball consisted of a leather case with a rubber bladder, pumped to the required size and weight. With a boot-lace join, these balls became heavier and heavier in wet weather, leaving both defenders and attackers with sore heads. Stitched panels were introduced by the late 1950s. Although the first white ball was used in 1951, it did not succeed brown until 1970. Law Two of the Rules of the Game now stipulates the ball cannot be a circumference of less than 70 cm (28 in) or less than 67.5 cm (27 in) and must weigh no more than 448 g (16 oz) or less than 392 g (14 oz).

The use of a white ball instead of a brown one became official in 1970.

Ball Control

The most essential skill for any player is the ability to control the ball. Control is needed to create the space to make a pass, to dribble or to shoot at goal. Poor ball control has been the downfall of many a player from the school playground to a World Cup Final.

THE CONTINENTALS and other foreign players show superb ball control on a regular basis, while English teams have historically based their game on hard work and determination.

Practice is the key, but there are six guiding principles to proper control:

- be relaxed
- get into line with the ball as quickly as possible
- decide which part of the body you will use to control the ball
- withdraw that part on impact to cushion the ball and take the pace off it
- control the ball to the side of your body to take second touch
- get your head up to make your next move

PASSING AND SHOOTING

THE BEST PASSERS of the ball tend to have the best control because their technique gives them that extra fleeting second to compose themselves and decide on the best option before striking a pass. Yet for a player to make a successful pass, team-mates need to run into positions to receive the ball. The great Liverpool team of the 1970s destroyed many a side with their simple philosophy of 'pass and move'. A player should pass the ball whenever a team-mate is in a better position to shoot, build an attack or clear their defensive lines. A player should shoot if no other player is in a better shooting position.

Diego Maradona demonstrating his incredible ball-control.

PASSING WITH THE INSIDE OF THE FOOT

THIS IS THE MOST COMMON method of passing and the first for the player to perfect. Until the ball can be struck accurately along the ground for short distances, there is little chance of success with other methods.

It is the most accurate but has a lack of power, which means it cannot be used to strike the ball over any real distance.

To complete a successful pass with the inside of the foot a player must:

- have the non-kicking foot alongside the ball pointing in the intended direction
- have the kicking foot at right angles to the body and the line of the ball
- keep the head down and over the ball
- keep a firm ankle to strike the ball cleanly in the centre

SWERVING THE BALL WITH THE INSIDE OF THE FOOT

A CRUCIAL SKILL for any player who needs to cross the ball to a team-mate. The ability to curl the ball away from defenders into the path of on-coming attackers has always been one of the most potent passes in the game. It is also a great skill to use at freekicks. England's David Beckham has perfected the art with hours of practice on the training ground.

1. Head down over the ball
2. Firm ankle to strike cleanly
3. kicking foot at right angles to the body and line of the ball
4. Non-kicking foot alongside the ball, pointing in the direction of the shot

The following is required to master this skill:

- the kicking foot strikes across the ball from inside to outside
- make contact with the ball with the side of the big toe and foot
- strike the middle of the ball off centre to keep it low; the non-kicking foot must be behind the ball
- make a proper follow through with the kicking foot to put spin on the ball
- keep head steady with eyes on the ball

PASSING OR SHOOTING WITH
THE OUTSIDE OF THE FOOT

AN ADVANCED TECHNIQUE which can give players a
crucial advantage over others. It can help a player perform
'flick' passes and swerve the ball around opponents. Brazil's
Roberto Carlos is one of the greatest exponents of this skill and
often employs it for long-range free-kicks.

It needs considerable work and the following
needs to be practised:

- for a flick pass, position the kicking foot inside
  the ball and flick the ball with an outward
  movement
- keep the ball down by striking its centre
- to swerve to the right, the kicking foot should
  strike across the ball just left of centre with an
  outside to inside movement. The same
  procedure should be used on the other side
  of the ball for the left swerve
- non-kicking foot should be a little behind and to
  the side of the ball
- keep the head steady and eyes on the ball

PASSING OR SHOOTING WITH THE INSTEP

THIS IS A MORE DIFFICULT SKILL, which is often
required when trying to pass the ball while running with it, or
when shooting or trying to drive the ball over long distances.
England's Alan Shearer is among the best in the business at
this technique.

To pass or shoot successfully with the instep along the ground a player must:

- have toes pointing down towards the ground
- strike the ball in the centre
- have non-kicking foot alongside the ball but a few centimetres to the side
- keep the head still with eyes on the ball

N.B. If a player strikes the ball while leaning back or with their non-kicking foot behind the side of the ball, it will fly off the ground when kicked.

THE LOFTED PASS

A PASS REGULARLY used by defenders trying to pick out forward players. The ball can be struck long distances, swiftly turning defence into attack. The aim is to make contact with the ball with the front of the foot. Frank Leboeuf of Chelsea and France is a fine exponent of this skill.

To execute a lofted pass successfully, the player must do the following:

- strike the central bottom half of the ball with the laces of the boot
- ensure non-kicking foot is level with the ball
- approach the ball at right angles to the direction in which you wish to pass. Running straight on will see the ball drift to the right or left because of the natural kicking motion
- develop a more pronounced backswing with the heel coming up towards the buttocks and the knee pointing towards the ball
- Keep the head steady and eyes on the ball

THE CHIP

ONE OF THE MOST pleasing passes to execute and potentially one of the most damaging to opponents. The ability to chip a ball over an outstretched leg or even over a jumping defender can open up great goalscoring opportunities. The chip puts great backspin on the ball, which can make distance difficult to judge. Germany's Franz Beckenbauer was a master of this technique.

It requires the following skills:

- stabbing the foot under the ball making contact with the big toe
- maintaining short back lift
- non-kicking foot 7-10 cm (3-4 in) to the side of the ball
- keep the head steady and eyes on the ball

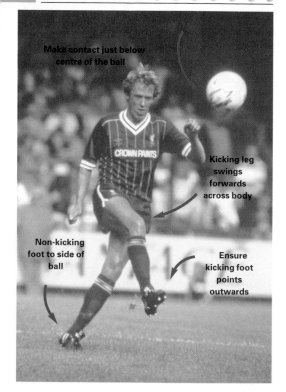

Make contact just below centre of the ball

Kicking leg swings forwards across body

Non-kicking foot to side of ball

Ensure kicking foot points outwards

VOLLEYING THE BALL

ONE OF THE MOST difficult skills to perfect, yet this is regularly required during the course of a game. Although deadly in attacking positions, it can be used anywhere on the pitch to get out of difficult situations. Mark Hughes of Wales, Manchester United and Chelsea has been one of the great volleyers of recent years.

To volley with the instep from a straight approach a player must:

- have the kicking foot pointing towards the ground
- strike through the middle bottom half of the ball
- keep the non-kicking foot behind the ball
- keep the eyes looking down at the ball with a steady head

To volley with the instep from a sideways approach a player must:

- ensure the kicking foot points outwards
- the kicking leg swings forward and across the body
- contact is made just below the centre of the ball
- the non-kicking foot is well to the side of the ball

Phil Neal of Liverpool volleys the ball.

DRIBBLING

THE ABILITY TO run with the ball past defenders at speed is still the most devastating skill any player can possess. England's Michael Owen earned rave reviews at the 1998 World Cup for possessing this talent, and all-time greats like Pele and Maradona have been blessed with this special skill.

Dribbling with the ball is essentially an attacking requirement. It can be dangerous if employed in defensive situations. The essential aim of dribbling is to run direct at defenders and throw them off balance with a feint or dummy to allow the attacking player to go past.

No matter how good the player, dribbling can often lead to losing the ball. When it works it can lead to a goal.

Some coaches claim that players are born with the ability to dribble. Yet like all other football skills, everyone can improve through practice.

Practising dribbling

Players should start by dribbling around a line of cones or objects. Build confidence and speed.

Practice throwing a feint e.g. dropping a shoulder one way

and moving off to the other.

Practice a dummy e.g. leg over the ball. Left leg over the ball, step inside and move ball away to the right.

The essential skills for dribbling are:

- close ball control
- balance
- change of pace
- strength
- awareness of defenders
- ability to feint and dummy

Maradona's dribbling skills made him one of the greatest players ever.

CROSSING

ANALYSIS OF MATCHES across the globe reveals that three-quarters of all goals scored come from crosses, so this is a key skill when it comes to forward play. The ability to cross a ball involves the use of various techniques outlined earlier. The ball can be crossed with the inside and outside of the foot or even volleyed. There is a wide range of crosses which can be deployed to keep defenders guessing.

Near Post

The ball is played in towards the post nearest the kicker. Normally struck at half-pace, it is played at head height and is intended to be met by an in-coming forward.

Near-post cross: player A plays the ball to the post nearest to him, his team-mate B feints to lose his marker (C) and meets the ball in the cross.

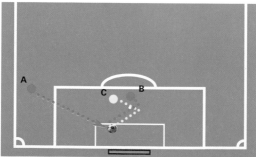

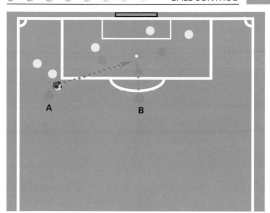

Centre-goal: Player A crosses the ball into the penalty area to meet a late run by player B: note the marking positions of the other team members.

Centre Goal

This needs to be played outside the 5.5 m (6 yd) goal area, otherwise the goalkeeper will claim it. The ideal area to aim for is around the penalty mark. This gives forwards a chance to win the ball and head for goal.

Far Post

A high cross over the goalmouth to the post furthest from the kicker. It should be high enough to clear the goalkeeper and defenders and is designed for powerful headers of the ball to attack.

Early cross

If a wide player has got behind the last defender on the flank, an early cross played behind central defenders into the path of incoming forwards can cause real damage.

Inswinging cross

An attacker may cut inside and cross a ball which moves towards the goal-line. These should be aimed high towards the far post eliminating defenders, teasing the goalkeeper and picking out attacking forwards running in from the other side of the pitch.

Hard and low

When the ball is driven hard and low across the penalty area, anything can happen. They are perfect for fast-reacting forwards and a nightmare for defenders, who run the risk of deflecting the ball into their own net.

Cut back

Fool defenders by getting past the last defender and then cut the ball back towards the edge of the penalty area rather than hitting a cross. This can wrong-foot defenders and allow forwards to benefit.

West Ham's Alan Sealey playing the ball hard and low in the penalty area.

Shooting

The ultimate skill in the game. If you do not shoot, you will not score goals and that is the whole object of the exercise. The one thing great goalscorers always achieve is to get their shots on target. They also tend to be selfish and rarely worry about missing! Being good at shooting often comes down to attitude. Do not be afraid to have a go and always put accuracy before power.

WHERE TO AIM

LOW SHOTS into the far corners of the goal are the hardest for the goalkeeper to reach because it gives them the greatest distance to cover. They can also take a deflection off another player or the pitch to cause further trouble. High shots are easier for a goalkeeper to judge and reach.

WHEN NOT TO SHOOT

WHILE PLAYERS SHOULD be encouraged to shoot as often as possible, there are times when a shot will simply surrender possession of the ball. Players should not shoot when an opponent is certain to block it, if the distance is so great that there is little chance of scoring or if the angle is so tight that it is unlikely that the target will be hit.

The following elements will all aid shooting success:

- practice
- composure
- accuracy
- looking where the goalkeeper is positioned
- head down

Low shots to the far corner of the goal are the most likely to succeed.

Heading

Heading does not come naturally to anyone. It can hurt at first and needs practice. However, for all players, it is an essential skill. The key elements to successful heading are timing and keeping the eyes on the ball. Different techniques are required for different types of headers, depending on whether the player is in an attacking or defensive situation.

ATTACKING HEADER

WHEN HEADING the ball in an attacking area, players are encouraged whenever possible to get above the ball so they can head it down into the ground towards goal. As with shooting, this is the hardest ball for a goalkeeper to reach.

DEFENSIVE HEADING

DEFENDERS ARE looking for height and distance when they are trying to clear their lines. In order to achieve this, it is essential to get under the line of flight of the ball so the ball can be headed up and away.

Above: Italian Serie A players head the ball.
Right: Defenders head the ball to gain height and distance.

Tackling

If shooting is the match-winning element of any game, tackling can often be the match-saver. To many spectators, and indeed team-mates, the sound and sight of a perfectly timed tackle can be as uplifting as a flash of forward brilliance. Timing and bravery are the key elements when it comes to tackling. If players back out they tend to get hurt.

THE BLOCK TACKLE

THIS IS THE MOST common tackle and is used to win the ball off an opponent. It needs good timing and use of the inside of the foot. The force of the foot needs to go through the centre of the ball with both knees flexed to absorb the impact.

SLIDING TACKLES

THE MOST DRAMATIC tackle and the most risky in the modern day when a mistimed challenge can lead to an automatic sending-off. To pull off a successful sliding tackle, players must keep their eyes on the ball and get as close to the ball as possible. The tackling leg should start off slightly ahead of the ball, otherwise the tackler is in danger of catching the opponent's leg and conceding a foul. The tackling leg also needs to be low and close to the ground to avoid injury.

Successful tackling is based on timing and courage.

Goalkeeping

The goalkeeper is without doubt the most important
member of a side. One mistake or one vital save by a
goalkeeper can mean the difference between
defeat or victory.

AGILITY, STRENGTH and bravery are the key requirements
of a good goalkeeper. Height obviously helps, as does age.
Many goalkeepers do not reach their full potential until they
are about 30. Peter Schmeichel of Manchester United and
England's David Seaman are amongst the best in the world.

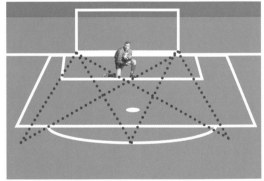

*Practise coming off the goal-line to narrow the angles from an attacking
shot; the size of the angles are shown here from different positions outside
the penalty box.*

PRACTICE

GOALKEEPING IS A SCIENCE in itself, but the basic principle involves getting the body or part of the body behind the ball at the earliest and every opportunity. It is important that goalkeepers are given specialist practice to help them sharpen their game. Practice in saving shots, narrowing angles, coming out for crosses, one-on-one situations with an attacker and kicking and throwing the ball are all essential for a goalkeeper to make the most of their abilities.

Peter Shilton, one of England's greatest goalkeepers.

Training

Like any physical sport, football places considerable
demands on the player at whatever level they are
performing. To get the most out of your own ability and
most enjoyment from the game, it is vital to have some
degree of basic fitness. It is also crucial when it comes
to avoiding serious injury.

WHY DO IT?

SOME OF THE most skilful players in the world have been
forced to retire earlier than expected because of their reluctance
to put in hard work in the gym or on the training field.
Others have kept playing at the highest level well into their
thirties – and on rare occasions forties – thanks to their
commitment to keeping fit.

N.B. Youngsters aged below 14 are not encouraged by coaches to
do any particular physical training. At that age you are naturally fit
and simply playing the game will keep you in condition.

TRAINING FOR YOUNG PLAYERS 11–14

THE BEST WAY FOR young players to practice is for them to
work individually with the ball. Many greats have honed their
skills by kicking the ball against a wall or juggling cans, and it is
this 'feel' for the ball which needs to be developed early on. The
Dutchman Wiel Coerver, regarded as the best youth coach in
the game, recommends boys have 6,000 touches of a ball a day!

Grobbelar and Lawrenson celebrate Liverpool's goal against Chelsea.

That is perhaps not realistic, but youngsters with dreams of going as far as they can in the game should try and practise in some form every day.

Ball Juggling

By juggling the ball with the feet, head, shoulders and knees, a player can develop an innate ability to keep the ball under control. Ability to control the ball is the most fundamental skill in football. Have competitions with friends to see who can juggle the ball for the longest.

Running With the Ball

The ability to run at defenders with
the ball under tight control is one
of the most productive talents any
player can possess. In the 1998
World Cup the likes of England's
Michael Owen and Holland's
Dennis Bergkamp were among the
most feared players on view.
Regular practice by running with
the ball round obstacles is great
preparation for the real thing. Once confident in beating
inanimate objects, do the same thing with real opponents.

Small-sided Games

Youngsters aged below 14 are not recommended to play in too
many matches on a full-size pitch. Instead they should play
games with no more than six-a-side on a smaller pitch. This
guarantees regular touches of the ball and involvement in the
action – the best way to develop a young player's interest.

TRAINING FROM 14–16

At this age the emphasis should still remain on developing
skills as outlined above, but young players can begin general
fitness training to build up leg strength and stamina. Beware of
talented young players being forced in to too many matches.
Some young stars of the past have been burned out by the age
of 18 and missed out on a potential professional career simply
by playing too much competitive football.

Michael Owen's runs with the ball are now well-known.

TRAINING TIPS

When to Train

This depends very much on what level you are playing, but everyone needs to keep fit for football. Any properly run club will have regular training sessions, varying from once a week to three or four times a week. Dedicated players maintain a high level of fitness and conditioning throughout the year, but the pre-season sessions are crucial in establishing a basic level of fitness for the season ahead.

How to Train

Training exercises should concentrate on developing two areas – stamina and sprinting.

Professional players keep up a high level of fitness all year round.

Building up Stamina

Take a 12-minute run round a course with each player's distance measured at of time allowed.

Go for a four-mile cross-country run, preferably through trees and with hill climbs. Individuals should be timed and encouraged to beat their existing time on the next run.

Interval training: players should line up in pairs on the edge of opposing penalty boxes. On the whistle, player one runs across the pitch to a colleague, who sets off while player one rests. Each player should make six runs.

Sprint, jog, walk session: on the instruction of the coach, players sprint, jog or walk round the pitch. Do two laps then walk for a minute. Repeat three times.

Sprinting (all done at full speed)

Shuttle runs: place cones at 5, 10, 15, 20 and 25 m (5, 11, 16, 21 and 27 yd). The player runs out to each cone and back in turn. Do three runs in the first session, building up to 10.

Doggies: the player runs 30 m (32 yd) and back three times, with 10 seconds rest in between.

Sprints 30-40-50-60-m (32-43-54-65 yd). In teams of three, player one runs to the 30-m (32-yd) marker and back, followed by players two and three. The first player then runs to the 40-m (43-yd) marker and so on.

Weight Training

Using weights is a great way of developing more speed and power, but it must be done under guidance from a qualified instructor. Incorrect use of weights can lead to serious injury. During the summer close season three sessions a week are perfect for maintaining muscle condition. During the season, two sessions are ideal if playing on Saturdays or Sundays only. Do not use weights until 48 hours after a game.

Warming-up is an essential part of playing and training.

Football Diet

The Continentals recognised long ago that correct diet has a direct effect on players' performance, but it has been slow to catch on in Britain, where steak and chips has been the staple diet of many great players.

IN RECENT YEARS, however, players have become much more careful about what they eat and drink. Fish, chicken and plenty of fruit and vegetables are a staple part of any athlete's diet, but high-protein foods such as meat, fish and dairy products should only be eaten at the start of a week before a game. High carbohydrates like pasta and potato help

build up energy and should be eaten in the days immediately before the match. Ideal foods to eat before a game: pasta, bread, potatoes or rice.

The best time to eat is three hours before a game and this should consist of foods such as cereals, toast or scrambled eggs, which provide high energy and can be digested easily. Up to kick-off time the player should aim to drink as much fluid (non-alcoholic!) as possible to combat the effects of dehydration.

Pre-match Routines

Every player has their own way of getting ready for a game but it is crucial some stretching exercises are carried out before kick-off. This warm-up should last about 20 minutes.

INITIALLY, perform stationary exercises to stretch out the muscles. Start from the feet and work upwards. Loosen the ankles by rotating them, and stretch the calves and thighs by bending and kicking the legs up behind you.

Next, work the groin and hamstring by putting feet wide apart and bending one knee to the side, so stretching the muscles. Repeat on both sides. Loosen back and stomach by touching toes with opposite hand.

Once stretches are complete, do some light jogging and running. You are now ready for the ball. Get a good feel for it and then work with team-mates.

Players performing stretching exercises before a match.

Avoiding and Treating Injuries

Around 80 professional players are forced to retire through injury each season – the majority have all the training and advice possible. Such assistance is rarely offered for amateurs. Players should look for clubs where someone with medical knowledge is on hand at matches.

PLAYERS CAN HELP themselves by following basic steps if they suffer an injury. More serious injuries need attention from a qualified doctor.

CUTS

WOUNDS MUST BE cleaned with antiseptic. It may be necessary to cover the wound although air will aid healing. Serious cuts should be attended by a qualified medical practitioner.

BLISTERS

THE SCOURGE OF PLAYERS when the ground is hard. Rubbing soft soap or Vaseline inside socks can reduce the friction that creates blisters.

BRUISES

ICE OR COLD compresses help reduce the swelling, except with deep-seated bruises which need the attention of an expert physiotherapist. Gentle stretching exercises can help recovery.

Cramp is one of the most common complaints among footballers.

CRAMP

THE BEST WAY of avoiding cramp is to train harder, but it happens to the fittest of players in particularly exhausting matches. The calf muscle is normally the worst affected. Treat it by lying down and straightening the leg with the toes raised and the heel pressed down. Come off the pitch if it persists.

CONCUSSION

IF A PLAYER APPEARS to be concussed, perform a simply eye test by asking them to look at a moving finger on the line of their nose. If there is any doubt about their vision, stop them playing and take them for a hospital check-up.

MUSCLES

HELP PREVENT muscle strain by conducting thorough warm-ups. If injury is sustained, gentle stretching helps recovery, but guidance is needed from a physiotherapist.

SPRAINS

A PLAYER SHOULD always leave the field if they have suffered a sprain, and ice should be applied to reduce the swelling. Immersion in hot and cold water alternately will help recovery and a strapping will be required. More serious sprains require an X-ray to establish whether there is any ligament damage.

Injuries can be avoided by careful warm-up routines.

Becoming a Coach

Many professional players aspire to coaching positions
once it is time for them to hang up their boots. The
same can be said of people in the amateur game.
The Football Association runs courses giving
would-be coaches tuition on the basics of
teaching football and how to get the best out of
players, be they young or old.

COURSES ARE OPEN to
anyone and professional
players will often be learning
alongside people who run local
youth or adult teams. Strict
standards are laid down and
only those reaching the required
level are granted an FA Prelim-
inary Coaching badge.

Delegates on the courses
all need to show a degree of
proficiency themselves. They
are taught how to develop
players' skills, how to set up
effective practices, how to
motivate and how to commun-
icate. They are tested on the
rules of the game and have to
show an ability to put coaching
principles into practice.

Qualified coaches who put their new-found knowledge to good use can later complete a further course and examination to win the FA's Full Coaching badge.

Left: Former Newcastle manager Kenny Dalglish.
Above: Dalglish's replacement at Newcastle, Ruud Gullit.

Becoming a Referee

When organised football started, the game was
marshalled by an umpire and a referee. In the 1880s,
touch judges were introduced to help with decisions,
and the triumvirate of referee and linesmen – who
today are known controversially as 'assistant
referees' – came into being shortly afterwards.

ROLE OF THE REFEREE

REFEREES ARE THE sole arbiters of the 17 laws of the game.
Their decisions can have crucial effects on the outcome of
matches and they are amongst the most controversial figures in
the sport. Their role has been the same from the very outset –
to ensure the smooth running of a game.

REFEREE'S KIT

THE APPEARANCE OF the 'man in black'
has remained fairly consistent. They
originally wore a jacket and plus-four
trousers, while the whistle was used for the
first time in 1878. Dark jackets and ties later
brought a greater sense of formality and
discipline to their role, and although these
items were later replaced by a black tunic and
black shorts, their uniforms remained sombre
until the 1990s. While FIFA still insists that
referees wear predominantly black kit for internationals,
English League referees have appeared resplendent in yellow
and even purple outfits.

While black remains the predominant colour for referees' kit,
some appear in brighter colours.

SKILLS OF A REFEREE

THE THOUGHT OF becoming a referee fills many players with absolute horror, yet without this key figure the game could not survive. The referee is responsible for making sure that the 17 laws of the game are enforced and has to make split-second judgements, which at the highest level are subjected to television scrutiny. More and more players are now learning how to become referees but more referees are needed at every level.

Experts claim that there are four essential requirements a referee needs to see fulfilled in a game:

- equality: so those who take part in the game have an equal opportunity to demonstrate individual skills.
- safety: in that the health of players must be safeguarded.
- enjoyment: whereby the game provides the maximum pleasure for all who take part.
- on top of that, they all need to apply that most personal and controversial trait – discretion.

Referees are responsible for the smooth running of the game.

Anyone can apply to become a referee, regardless of whether they have played the game themselves. The FA runs courses for aspiring referees. Delegates are given instruction on the laws of the game and practise controlling matches.

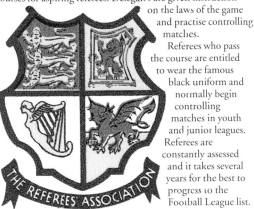

Referees who pass the course are entitled to wear the famous black uniform and normally begin controlling matches in youth and junior leagues. Referees are constantly assessed and it takes several years for the best to progress to the Football League list.

FITNESS REQUIREMENTS

REFEREES NEED TO be as fit, if not fitter, than the players. They have to keep up with play for the entire game in order to get the best angles to make the right decisions. A referee who struggles for fitness is more likely to make an error of judgement. Stamina is the key requirement and training programmes should be devised accordingly.

Symbol of the Referees' Association.

POSITIONS, FORMATIONS AND TACTICS

Positions

No positions, formations or tactics existed in the early days of football. The game basically amounted to hordes of players running after the ball in a haphazard fashion. No-one had a set position. There was no real method to the madness. The best players were those who could dribble and run with the ball at speed, a skill which is still one of the most effective in the modern game.

GOALKEEPER

THE ONE PERSON who is allowed to use his hands on the pitch. Goalkeeping is a specialist position where agility and bravery are the key requirements. It has been said that over a season a top goalkeeper can be worth 15 points to a team in a season, and that all the best sides through the years have tended to have the best goalkeepers.

FULL-BACK

ORIGINALLY this role was the last line of defence for a side. Players who were tough and strong in the tackle were the best for the job. In recent years they have needed to develop an ability to pass and cross the ball, as the full-back role has become one of the most versatile on the pitch.

Left: workmen's lunch-hour football; early football had few rules or tactics.
Above: ex-England goalkeeper Peter Shilton.

WING-BACK

IN THE LATE 1990s, some teams have dispensed with full-backs altogether and now use wing-backs. These players, often converted wingers, are required to attack and defend along the length of the pitch. It is hard work, but wing-backs are rarely out of the action.

CENTRE-BACK

THE CENTRE-BACK has been at the heart of any defence since the 1920s. Strong and brave, they are good at heading the ball and often organise the whole defence. Many centre-backs become captains because of their commanding presence. Since the 1950s the role has developed considerably. Centre-backs are now expected to show skill on the ball and the ability to turn defence into attack with pinpoint passing.

SWEEPER/LIBERO

THIS ROLE WAS introduced by the Italians in the late 1950s. It involved deploying a player behind the normal line of defence as extra cover. It was initially an entirely defensive role, but the great Franz Beckenbauer showed in the late 1960s how the 'libero' could spring out of defence and join the attack to catch opponents out. The role is now used regularly by many top sides.

Centre-back Tony Adams.

MIDFIELDER

PREVIOUSLY KNOWN as right-half, centre-half or left-half, midfielders form a team's 'engine room'. Providing the crucial link between defence and attack, the best midfield players have to display many attributes. They need to be skilful, good at passing, strong in the tackle, good headers of the ball and, most importantly, have bags of stamina.

STRIKER/FORWARD

AS THE NAME suggests, these players' primary role is basic – to score goals. In times gone by, centre-forwards would lurk upfield, taking little part in the action apart from when their side was attacking – hence the playground phrase 'goal hanger'. Strikers are now required to do their share of defensive work as well, but their success is still measured in terms of how many goals they have scored.

WINGER

ONE OF THE most exciting sights in the game is that of a speedy winger flying down the flank past a defender to cross the ball for a team-mate. Historically wingers have been amongst the most skilful members of a side – and in many cases the most timid! The skill factor can still apply today, but the game's modern demands insist these players also learn how to tackle and defend.

Left: England striker Alan Shearer.
Right: German full-back Markus Babbel during Euro 96.

Formations

As rules became standardised towards the latter half of
the nineteenth century, teams gradually stopped
consisting of players chasing the ball; instead
becoming organised formations. These are some of
the most common formations used in the game.

1-1-8

ONCE PLAYERS STOPPED attacking *en masse*, the first
basic formation of 1-1-8 came into being – full-back, half-back
and eight forwards! The system was simple in the extreme.
Attack was clearly the best form of defence.

2-2-6

IT WAS THE GREAT Scottish side Queen's Park who brought some sophistication to the game. They were the first team to 'pass' the ball in any true sense, which meant the game, which had previously moved up and down the centre of the pitch, began to cover the entire playing area.

They developed a formation of 2-2-6, consisting of two full-backs, two half-backs and six attackers.

2-3-5

IN 1867 THE offside law changed, stating that a player was offside only if less than three defenders were between them and the goal-line at the time the ball was played. When that happened, it paved the way for a 2-3-5 system: two full-backs, three half-backs and five forwards. This system operated successfully for the better part of 50 years.

2-3-5 formation.

3-2-2-3

IN THE LATE 1920s, the Arsenal captain, Charlie Buchan, and the legendary manager, Herbert Chapman, made a significant change in an attempt to combat the flood of goals being scored. The centre-half moved back to play between the two full-backs, and two forwards were pulled into midfield positions. Two half-backs and three forwards were deployed. The 'WM' formation– 3-2-2-3 – was born. This system, with some minor variations, was universally employed for almost 30 years.

1-4-3-2

THE DEFENCE-conscious Italians were among the first to introduce the role of the 'sweeper' into the game. This defender was placed behind a line of four defenders. The role was quite simplistic – to stop any attackers who had breached the line of defenders in front of them. What was gained in defence was

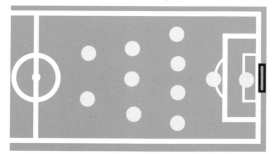

1-4-3-2 formation.

inevitably lost in attack, and although the Italians have persisted with variations on this theme, it has contributed to what some consider to be the sterile nature of their game.

4-2-4

THE BRILLIANT Hungarians of the 1950s invented the 4-2-4 system of four defenders, two half-backs and four forwards, and wreaked havoc on the the rest of Europe who were still predominantly employing the 3-2-2-3 formation developed by Arsenal.

In England and elsewhere, the centre-forward had been the linchpin of any attack, but the 'Magic Magyars' pulled their centre-forward into a deeper midfield role and had two inside-forwards and two wingers playing in attack. They also put one of the wing-halves into a central defensive position to introduce a four-man defence for the first time.

4-2-4 formation.

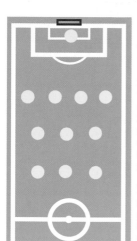

4-3-3

BRAZIL INTRODUCED this system in the late 1950s and it helped take them to three World Cup victories in 12 years. Displaying a rare flash of defensive inspiration, they simply pulled one of the forwards playing under the 4-2-4 system into a midfield role, so creating a line-up of four defenders, three midfielders and three forwards.

With the likes of Pele, Rivelino, Jairzinho and Tostao to make the system work, it produced some of the best football ever seen and was adopted across the world.

4-4-2

SIR ALF RAMSEY'S England won the 1966 World Cup playing what appears to be a defensive 4-4-2 formation of four defenders, four midfielders and two forwards. It was largely based on the great English footballing principles of effort and hard work.

Wingers were superfluous to requirements with midfielders encouraged to get 'up and down' the pitch, joining the attack

4-3-3 formation.

and then helping the defence. As with the Brazilian 4-3-3 formation, overlapping full-backs were encouraged. Under this system the defensive four tend to maintain their positions and push up the field to 'squeeze' the play into the opponents' half.

It has had its critics, but remains in regular use today. It gives teams a solid defensive platform but requires high work-rate and good team-work to be effective.

Above: Sir Alf Ramsey. Below: 4-4-2 formation.

1-4-4-1

THIS IS PERHAPS THE most defensive-minded system which can be used. It consists of sweeper, four defenders, four midfielders and a lone attacker. The Soviet and Russian sides used this tactic to good effect in the late 1980s and early 1990s.

By deploying a sweeper behind the four defenders, it makes a team very difficult to break down. Any mistakes by the defenders should be covered by the extra defensive player.

However, it places a great burden on the lone striker, who has to have great ability to control and hold the ball long enough for players to join the attack from midfield.

In this system, the lone striker does not have a tremendous defensive burden. The intention is that they concentrate on what they do best – scoring goals. Tottenham's Clive Allen proved the point under Pleat when in one season he scored 40 goals in the role.

1-4-4-1 formation

3-5-2

IT LOOKS DEFENSIVE with three defenders, five midfielders and two attackers, but, unlike most modern systems, allows attack-minded players to display their talents. Used by England at the 1998 World Cup, many teams have adopted this pattern of play in recent seasons.

Sides line up with a sweeper playing behind two centre-backs. The full-backs have pushed in to a wing-back role where they are given licence to attack.

The three central midfielders include at least one player who will adopt a 'holding role' just in front of the centre-backs. The other two will be free to join attacks whenever possible.

The two attackers need the ability to hold the ball up for other players to join in an attacking move. They roam across the whole width of the pitch in forward positions, attempting to create a place for their strike partner or midfield colleagues.

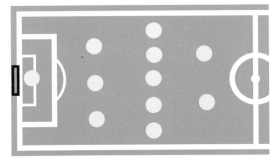

3-5-2 formation.

Tactics

Tactics are defined in the dictionary as: 'the science and art of disposing of and manoeuvring forces in combat'. No wonder then that although football is a highly instinctive and simple game, tactical awareness from coaches in the modern day has taken the game to a new dimension.

BACKGROUND

A FLASH OF INDIVIDUAL inspiration will often change the course of a match, but at the highest level teams compile extensive dossiers on the way their opponents are likely to play, in a bid to find some kind of edge. The information will include analyses of formations, which foot players prefer, how they line up for free-kicks and corners and the opposing side's strengths and weaknesses.

Top coaches and managers will then devise tactics for each game, aimed at exposing the opponents' deficiencies and combating their strengths. By their very nature, tactics are constantly evolving and more than one leading coach has been forced to re-think their approach within a few moments of a game starting, due to their opposing number springing a surprise in the line-up.

As the 1998 World Cup showed when England manager Glenn Hoddle refused to name his team until the last moment, football in the modern day is as much a game of chess off the pitch as it is on the field of play.

England manager during the 1998 World Cup, Glenn Hoddle.

Attacking Moves

The hardest route to goal is through the middle. Defenders are trained to deflect attacks out to the flanks where there is less space for forwards. Speed of thought and movement is the key to breaking through the heart of a defence.

IF A PLAYER has possession of the ball, he has a choice of whether to pass, dribble or shoot. If within an appropriate range a shot should be encouraged, otherwise the player should be seeking to pass the ball to a team-mate in a better position.

That means it is essential for players who do not have the ball to run in to space, preferably behind defenders. To be truly effective as an attacking force, a team needs to commit players forward. In these defence-minded days there is sometimes a reluctance to take a gamble which could end up with the opponents winning possession, exploiting the space left at the back and scoring at the other end.

MAKING SPACE

IN ORDER to create space, forwards must never be still or run in straight lines. To fool defenders, they should move off in one direction but then cut back the other way to receive the ball. The best strikers will invariably make diagonal runs to create angles for their team-mates. Forwards, however, should vary their running patterns so defenders do not begin to predict the next move.

Right: Italian Di Matteo takes on opposition defenders.

BLIND-SIDE RUNS

THIS IS A SIMPLE and effective technique of running
into the space behind a defender whose attention has been
taken with the ball. It provides an attacker in possession
with the perfect opportunity to play a pass and create a goal-
scoring opportunity.

OVERLAP RUNS

THESE ARE commonplace in the modern game, with full-backs and wing-backs prepared to race forwards beyond a player in possession to make space for a pass. England's Graeme Le Saux is a fine exponent of this technique, which requires a high level of fitness and confidence. Key requirements are good communication between the overlapping player and player in possession, and timing, so that the overlapping player does not run offside. The pass must be played ahead of the overlapping player so he takes it in his stride, while the overlapping player needs to deliver a good final pass or cross to make the move worthwhile!

THE WALL PASS

THIS IS ONE of the most effective and most common ways of beating defenders in any part of the field, but particularly when it comes to attacking areas where defenders are reluctant to retreat. A player in possession when confronted by a defender simply passes the ball on a diagonal line to a team-mate, runs past the defender and receives a return pass after running past the opponent. It amounts to bouncing a ball off a wall and collecting the return – hence its name. Timing is the key. Releasing the pass too early or too late will allow the defender to recover their position.

Right: England's Michael Owen, in the 1998 World Cup.

ROTATING

THIS INVOLVES players interchanging positions in man-to-man marking situations to drag opponents into unfamiliar areas of the pitch. The great Dutch side of the 1970s and early 1980s did this constantly with their 'total football' approach, which saw defenders popping up in attack and attackers working in defence. The idea is to disrupt the defensive game plan of the opposing team and thus create holes in their organisation to exploit.

RUNNING WITH THE BALL

PLAYERS SHOULD BE encouraged to run with the ball when space opens up in front of them. It gets defenders back-pedalling and can gain vital metres in seconds. With English defences playing the tight game of the modern day, it is often difficult to find an opportunity for a clear run, but when the occasion does arise, players should go for it at speed. Do not have too many touches while running with the ball because that slows down the pace of the attack. However, ensure that the ball is not too far ahead otherwise possession will be lost. Eyes should be looking ahead, not down.

Michel Platini running into an open space with the ball.

TURNING WITH THE BALL

ONE OF THE most difficult things to achieve in football is to receive the ball with your back to the goal, and turn while a defender is breathing down your neck. Players who are able to turn in these tight situations (and shoot) are often the most sought after. The player needs an accurate, firm pass to their feet. They can then either drag the ball back with the inside of a foot, pivot on the standing leg and get a shot in or control the ball with the outside of the foot, swivel and take a shot.

England's Alan Shearer is a modern master at this, while ex-Liverpool star Kenny Dalglish was among the very best.

TARGET MAN

A TEAM CAN only use the long pass to turn defence into attack if they have a forward with the ability to work as a target man. These players need to have good close control so they can receive a well-hit pass and retain possession long enough for team-mates to join them in support. They also have to be good in the air so they can outjump defenders to head the ball on to colleagues.

There needs to be good understanding between the defender making the pass and the forward, who needs to move away from his marker on a diagonal route in order to create space.

Above: Alan Shearer, the master at turning with the ball.

Kenny Dalglish celebrates his goal, Liverpool vs. Chelsea, 1986.

Defensive Moves

Defending is all about reducing the amount of time, space or options an attacking player has when they are in possession. To be an effective defence, every member of the team needs to share the responsibility. Coaches will always tell strikers that they are the first line of defence when possession is lost.

DEFENDERS NEED high levels of concentration, patience, courage and self-discipline. As referees are given ever-greater instruction to assist the attacking players, the role of a defender is not an easy one.

PREVENTING AN OPPONENT TURNING

DEFENDERS WHO ALLOW an opponent to turn are in danger of being by-passed, so preventing this is a crucial skill to develop. The best way to stop a forward turning is to remember the first commandment of defending, namely: 'stay on your feet'.

Do not get too close to the attacking play. One metre (1 yd) is ideal: far enough away to see the ball but near enough to make a challenge if the player tries to turn. Remember to watch the ball rather than the opponent and be patient. It is down to the attacker to get past; the defender does not have to act. The moment to pounce is when the attacker is half-turned.

The best time for a defender to make his move is when the attacker is half turned.

HOLDING UP AN ATTACK

THERE WILL BE many times in a game when an attacker receives the ball facing the opponents' goal. In this situation the defender must try to get the attacker to pass backwards or sideways. This can be achieved by getting between the ball and the goal as quickly as possible while remaining well-balanced in order to react to sudden changes of direction. By 'holding up' the attacker in this way, it gives team-mates more time to get back and provide further cover. The defender can try and gain the initiative by feinting to tackle, but must not commit to a tackle unless the ball is there for the taking.

FORCING PLAY

THERE ARE TWO directions a defender should look to force an attacker – either down the touchline or across the field. This is achieved by adopting a position on a diagonal line about 4 m (4 yd) in front of an attacker, which prevents them cutting inside or passing inside. If the defender is trying to force an attacker to the right, they should move to their right, or vice-versa for the left. Defenders should try and force attackers into narrow spaces or areas where there are more defenders.

Defenders can feint a tackle in 'holding up' an attack.

BLOCKING A WALL PASS

IF AN ATTACKER tries to by-pass a defender by using the wall pass outlined earlier, the defender should ignore the ball and go with the runner to cut off the chance of a return pass.

PRESSURING AN OPPONENT

THIS IS A DEFENSIVE requirement for every player on the field. Teams will adopt their own approach, but as a general rule the nearest player should close down an opponent with the ball. This means getting in between the player and the goal and, without making a tackle, trying to force the opponent into a mistake.

On some occasions teams will let opponents who have been identified as having a weakness receive the ball so they can be pressurised into an error. The same approach is sometimes adopted when it comes to letting opponents have possession unchallenged in deep-lying areas of the pitch, to allow a team to re-group.

Few teams can maintain a high-pressurising game for 90 minutes, so coaches who adopt this tactic will use it in short bursts, often at the start of each half and after a goal has been scored.

PRESSING

THIS IS AIMED at pressing the game into the opponents' half. The defensive unit will push right up to the halfway line and deny the opposition any forward space in which to play. The move transfers play away from a team's own goal and puts opponents on the back foot. However, it is susceptible to counter-attack if the opposing team have a speedy forward who can run from their own half, or if they have a player with an eye for a long pass.

It is defender's job to pressure the opponent, forcing him to make a mistake.

THE SCREEN

AS FORMATIONS have developed in recent years, more and more players are being used as a defensive shield in front of the back line of defenders. This type of player is normally a midfielder who is good at passing the ball and tenacious in the tackle. Their role is to break up opponents' attacks before they reach the danger zone and to collect the ball from defenders and get attacking movements underway. This role has often been adopted by Paul Ince for England.

MAN-FOR-MAN MARKING

TEAMS WILL ADOPT this tactic in an attempt to nullify a key opposing player. It involves a player shadowing an opponent around the pitch wherever they go. It takes great concentration and dedication but can be invaluable in snuffing out a dangerous player.

Marking involves shadowing the opponent wherever they go on the pitch.

ZONAL DEFENDING

THIS APPROACH is adopted by the majority of clubs in the English League. It involves lining up with a back four in which every defender is responsible for picking up and marking an opponent who comes into their zone. If the attacking player moves into another defender's zone, it is down to the next defender to take over the marking role. Each defender should provide cover to their nearest colleague. For instance, if the attacking play comes down the right, the back four should move to the right. If the play moves down the centre of the field, the full-backs move inside to help the centre-backs push the attackers out to the flanks. It requires good defensive awareness and communication between defenders.

THE SWEEPER SYSTEM

THIS HAS BEEN used by the Continentals for years and is finally taking hold in the British game. A sweeper normally operates between two or three fellow defenders who have been given man-to-man marking responsibilities. As the 'free' player behind the defence it is the job of the sweeper to intercept any passes over the top and to challenge any players breaking through on goal. The presence of a sweeper allows defenders to make more attempts to tackle, as they know there is some back-up behind them if they fail. The system's main weakness can be exposed by hard-running strikers who can pull the man-to-man markers out of position and create space for other forwards.

DEFENDING FREE-KICKS

IT IS THE RESPONSIBILITY of the goalkeeper to position the defensive wall when free-kicks are awarded in dangerous areas. More players are needed the nearer the ball is to the goal. One member of the wall should be in communication with the goalkeeper to make sure it is properly aligned. The wall should be lined up with the first player standing a metre (yard) outside the line of the post nearest to the ball. An extra player should be detailed to run out and try and block the ball after it is struck.

DEFENDING CORNERS

GOALKEEPERS HAVE TO BE in charge of their penalty area and they will normally choose to have players covering both posts during a corner kick. Defenders given this job should stand approximately 1 m (1 yd) inside the post so that they are able to move in both directions to cover the area. They must ensure that they do not block the goalkeeper's line of vision. Goalkeepers should aim to claim any ball played into their 5.5 m (6 yd) area. They need to stand 1 metre (1 yard) off the goal-line and adopt a fairly central position in the goal so they can make ground in any direction depending on the flight of the ball.

The goalkeeper should position the defensive wall before a free-kick is taken.

Re-start Tactics

GOAL-KICKS

GOALKEEPERS SHOULD practise their kicking to make sure their clearances set up attacking opportunities, rather than present the opposition with the ball.

The throw-in is the most common way of restarting the game.

There are three options for kicks from the 5.5 m (6 yd) box:

- aim at a forward player who is strong in the air who will be supported by team-mates for a flick on or knockdown
- aim towards an opposing full-back who, under pressure from a forward, is likely to surrender possession
- pass to a defender who has dropped back to receive the ball

The same approaches can be adopted for kicks out of the hands, although if a long ball is being played it is essential the team in possession push as far upfield as possible, in order to put their opponents under pressure.

THROW-INS

MANY TEAMS STRUGGLE to retain possession at a throw-in, yet it is the most regular re-start in the game. The quicker a throw is taken, the more likely a team is to retain possession. Whenever possible, the ball should be thrown forward to a player who has created space and is unmarked. When taking a throw in their own half, players should look to 'work' the ball along the line, gaining vital distance and moving the danger away from their own penalty area.

Long throws can be a useful attacking weapon, as England's Gary Neville showed at the 1998 World Cup. The harder and lower the throw, the more dangerous it becomes for an opposing defender. The most difficult throw for a team to combat is the one to the near post, where attackers lurk for a flick on or shot at goal.

FREE-KICKS

PRACTICE MAKES PERFECT, as David Beckham shows regularly for Manchester United and England. If in range, it is always worth having a shot at goal. Two players, one right-footed and one left-footed, should be involved to confuse the defending side.

It is crucial that the ball is struck at the right pace. Too slow, and the goalkeeper will have time to react. Too hard, and it will sail over the bar. To deceive the defence, one player should run over the ball a split second before the kick is taken. Other attackers should be ready to react in case the ball is deflected towards them.

If the free-kick is in a wide position, the attacking team has a choice of striking an inswinging or outswinging cross. As a rule, if the defence has pushed out towards the edge of the penalty area, an outswinging cross is the answer, while if they are nearer to the goal, an inswinging ball can cause trouble in a crowded area.

CORNER-KICKS

ACCURACY IS the key requirement at corner-kicks and this is where players of all levels often let their team-mates down. Practice is the key ingredient and teams should develop a pattern of signals so attackers know what sort of corner is to be delivered.

A corner driven hard is more difficult for defenders to deal with than one that floats, and the corner-kick to the near-post is probably the most effective as it is the toughest for the goalkeeper to reach. The ball should be played with pace at head height, for a forward to flick on into the path of other forwards racing into the 5.5 m (6 yd) area.

A properly struck outswinging corner can also cause a defence trouble, although it can be difficult for attacking players to get the timing right to produce an effective effort on goal. In recent seasons, England's Teddy Sheringham has perfected this, meeting the outswinging corner with a volley at the edge of the area.

PENALTIES

THE KEY THING for a player taking a penalty is to make up their mind what they are going to do with the ball and then stick to the decision. Well-struck shots, low or high into the corner, are the hardest for a goalkeeper to reach, and that should be the penalty taker's prime objective. Then it is simply a case of conquering nerves and the pressure of the moment – as certain top players can testify!

Confidence is all important for the penalty taker.

Glossary

Advantage: Referee can waive foul if fouled team will benefit.

Assistant Referee: Formerly known as linesman.

'Black Panther': Nickname of great Portuguese player Eusebio.

Blind-side: Position on opposite side of an opponent to the ball.

'Busby Babes': Nickname for 1950s Manchester United team.

By-line: The goal-line.

Cambridge Rules: The game's first set of rules drawn up in 1848.

Campynge: Early Suffolk name for game similar to football.

Cautions: Punishment given to player for serious or persistent foul play.

Centre-back: Centrally positioned defender.

Chip: Quickly lifting the ball into the air.

Continentals: European-based teams and players.

Corner-kick: Awarded to attacking team when ball kicked over by-line by defender.

Cross: Ball played to a team-mate from a wide position.

Cut back: Ball played back from goal-line at sharp angle.

Dehydration: Lack of fluid in body leading to headaches and nausea.

Direct free-kick: Awarded for serious infringement of the rules.

Doggies: In training, player runs 30 m (32 yd) and back three times with 10 seconds rest in between.

Dribble: Attacker taking the ball past a defender.

Dummy: Feinting to move in one direction and going the other to trick a defender.

'Engine room': Nickname for unit of midfield players.

Extra-time: 30 mins added when teams are level after normal time.

FA Cup: World's oldest knockout football competition.

FA Premiership: New league introduced in 1992 involving top 22 clubs in England.

Far Post: Goal post furthest from the ball.

FIFA: International Federation of Association Football. Governing body for the game worldwide.

Football Association (The): Governing body in England.

Football League list: Panel of referees and assistants who officiate professional matches in England.

Forcing play: Pushing opponents in one direction.

Formation: Way a team lines up.

Foul: Breach of the Laws of the Game.

Full-back: Player in wide defending position.

Goal area: 5.5 m (6 yd) area drawn from goal posts.

Goal hanger: Slang for a forward who rarely runs back to defend.

Goal-kick: Awarded to defending team when ball kicked over goal-line by attacker.

Golden Goal: Goal which ends a match in extra-time.

'Hand of God': Description of goal when Diego Maradona punched ball into net.

Harpastum: Roman game which provided football's early origins.

Holding role: Player positioned in front of defenders.

Indirect free kick: Awarded for less serious offences.

Instep: Inner surface of the foot.

International Board: Law-making body attached to FIFA.

Interval training: Brief rests between bursts of running.

'Kaiser': Nickname for former West Germany captain Franz Beckenbauer.

Kenatt: Japanese game thought to be early predecessor of football.

'Kick and rush': Nickname for style played by Wolverhampton Wanderers in 1950s.

Kick-off: Start of a match, or re-start after half-time and after a goal is scored.

Libero: Another name for sweeper.

'Magic Magyars': Nickname for Hungarian national team in 1950s.

Man-for-man marking: Marking one opponent exclusively.

Mark: Follow an opponent to prevent them receiving the ball.

Midfielder: Player in central position.

Near Post: Goal post nearest the ball.

Obstruction: Blocking an opponent's path.

Offside: See under Laws of the Game.

'Old Invincibles': Nickname for Preston North End in 1880s.

Overlap: Run outside and beyond a team-mate.

Pass: Propelling ball to team-mate.

Pass and move: System of play developed by Liverpool.

Penalty: Awarded if attacking player is fouled in the penalty area.

Penalty area: 16.5 m (18 yd) area marked around the goal.

Penalty shootout: Sudden death way of deciding drawn matches.

Pre-match: Before a game.

Referee: Person responsible for interpreting play and imposing Laws of the Game.

Rotating: Players interchanging positions on the field.

Screen: Player positioned in front of defence to break up attacks early.

Shuttle runs: In training, running backwards and forwards between set distances.

Skill: Use of correct technique on demand.

Small-sided games: Practice matches in small groups.

Space: Increasing the distance between opponents.

Sprint: Running at full speed.

Squeeze: Pushing opponents back into confined space.

Stamina: Ability to maintain physical effort over long periods.

Striker: Forward player; chief responsibility to score goals.

Sweeper: Defending position introduced by Italians in 1960s.

Tackle: Challenge with the feet to win the ball.

Tactics: Methods of play used to beat opponents.

Target man: Striker used to receive long passes from defence.

Technique: Performance of a skill.

Throw-in: Awarded when the ball crosses the touchline.

Total football: Playing system invented by Holland in 1970s.

Touch judges: Forerunners of linesmen and assistant referees.

Touchline: Line marking the side of the pitch.

UEFA: Union of European Football Associations.

Up and down: Running from one end of the pitch to the other.

Volley: Kicking the ball before it bounces.

Wall pass: Pass between two players to exclude a defender.

WM formation: English system used in early twentieth century.

Weight training: Using weights to aid muscle development.

Wing-back: Wide positioned player who defends and attacks.

'Wizard of Dribble': Nickname for England's Stanley Matthews.

Zonal defending: System of defence where defenders mark opponents in defined areas of the pitch.

Useful Addresses

COUNTY FOOTBALL ASSOCIATIONS

Bedfordshire
P.D. Brown, Century House, Skimpot Road, Dunstable, LU5 4JU.

Berks and Bucks
B. Moore, 15a London Street, Faringdon, Oxon, SN7 8AG.

Birmingham County
M. Pennick, County FA Offices, Ray Hall Lane, Great Barr, Birmingham B43 6JE.

Cambridgeshire
R.K Pawley, 3 Signet Court, Swanns Road, Cambridge CB5 8LA.

Cheshire
A. Collins, The Cottage, Hartford Moss Recreation Centre, Winnington, Northwich CW8 4BG.

Cornwall
B.Cudmore, 1 High Cross Street, St Austell, Cornwall, PL25 4AB.

Cumberland
A. Murphy, 17 Oxford Street, Workington, Cumbria, CA14 2AL.

Derbyshire
K. Compton, The Grandstand, Moorways Stadium, Moor Lane, Derby, DE2 8FB.

Devon County
C. Davidson, Coach Road, Newton Abbott, Devon, TQ12 1EJ.

Dorset County
P. Hough, County Ground, Blandford Close, Harmworthy, Poole, Dorset, BH15 4BF.

Durham
J.Topping, 'Codeslaw', Ferens Park, Durham City, DH1 1JZ.

East Riding County
D.R. Johnson, 52 Bethune Avenue, Hull, HU4 7EJ.

Essex County
P. Sammons, 31 Mildmay Road, Chelmsford, Essex, CM2 0DN

Gloucestershire
P. Britton, Oaklands Park, Almondsbury, Bristol, BS12 4AG.

Guernsey
D. Dorey, Haut Regard, St Clair Hill, St Sampsons, Guernsey, GY2 4DT.

Hampshire
R.G. Barnes, 8 Ashwood Gardens, Off Winchester Road, Southampton SO16 7PW.

Herefordshire
J. Lambert, 1 Muirfield Close, Holmer, Hereford, HR1 1QB.

Hertfordshire
R.G. Kibble, 4 The Wayside, Leverstock Green, Hemel Hempstead, Herts., HP3 8NR.

Huntingdonshire
M.M. Armstrong, 1 Chapel End, Great Giddings, Huntingdon, Cambs., PE17 5NP.

Isle of Man
Mrs A. Garrett, PO Box 53, The Bowl, Douglas, Isle of Man.

Jersey
S. Monks, Rocquebery View, La Rue de Samares, St Clement, Jersey.

Kent County
K.T. Masters, 69 Maidstone Road, Chatham, Kent, ME4 6DT.

Lancashire
J. Kenyon, 31a Wellington Street, St John's, Blackburn, Lancs., BB1 8AU.

Leicestershire and Rutland
R.E. Barston, Holmes Park, Dog and Gun Lane, Whetstone, Leicester LE8 3LJ.

Lincolnshire
J.L. Griffin, PO Box 26, 12 Dean Road, Lincoln, LN2 4DP.

Liverpool County
F.L.J. Hunter, 23 Greenfield Road, Old Swann, Liverpool L13 3BN.

London
D. Fowkes, Aldworth Grove, London, SE13 6HY.

Manchester County
P. J. Smith, Sports Complex, Brantingham Road, Chorlton, Manchester, M21 1TG.

Middlesex County
P.J. Clayton, 39 Roxborough Road, Harrow, Middx., HA1 1NS.

Norfolk County
R. Howlett, J.P., Plantation Park, Blofield, Norwich, NR13 4PL.

Northamptonshire
B. Walden, 2 Duncan Close, Red House Road, Moulton Park, Northampton, NN3 1WL.

North Riding County
M. Jarvis, 284 Linthorpe Road, Middlesborough TS1 3QU.

Northumberland
R.E. Maughan, Seymour House, 10 Brenkley Way, Blezard Business Park, Seaton Barn, Newcastle upon Tyne, NE13 6DT.

Nottinghamshire
M.P. Kilbee, 7 Clarendon Street, Nottingham, NG1 5HS.

Oxfordshire
P.J. Ladbrook, 3 Wilkins Road, Cowley, Oxford, OX4 2HY.

Sheffield and Hallamshire
G. Thompson, Clegg House, 5 Onslow Road, Sheffield, S11 7AF.

Shropshire
D. Rowe, Gay Meadow, Abbey Foregate, Shrewsbury, SY2 6AB.

Somerset
Mrs H. Marchment, 30 North Road, Midsomer Norton, Bath, BA3 2QQ.

Staffordshire
B.J Adshead, County Showground, Weston Road, Stafford ST18 0DB

Suffolk County
W.M. Steward, 2 Millfields, Haughley, Suffolk IP14 3PU.

Surrey County
A.P. Adams, 321 Kingston Road, Leatherhead, Surrey, KT22 7TU.

Sussex County
D.M. Worsfold, County Office, Culver Road, Lancing, Sussex, BN15 9AX.

Westmorland
P. Ducksbury, 1 Dalton Road, Kendal, Cumbria, LA9 6AG.

West Riding County
R. Carter, Fleet Lane, Woodlesford, Leeds LS26 8NX.

Wiltshire
E.M. Parry, 44 Kennet Avenue, Swindon, SN2 3LG.

Worcestershire
M.R. Leggett, Fermain, 12 Worcester Road, Eynsham, Worcs., WR11 4JU.

NATIONAL FOOTBALL ASSOCIATIONS

The Football Association, 16 Lancaster Gate, London W2 3LW

The Irish FA, 20 Windsor Avenue, Belfast BT9 6EG

The Scottish Football Association, 6 Park Gardens, Glasgow G3 7YE

The Welsh Football Association, 3 Westgate Street, Cardiff, South Glamorgan CF1 1JF

Bibliography

Rothmans Football Yearbook 1997–98. Queen Anne Press (London, 1997).

News of the World Football Annual 1997–98. Invincible Press (London, 1997).

The Ultimate Encyclopaedia of Soccer. Carlton/Hodder & Stoughton (London, 1996).

Soccer Rules, Ken Goldman. Blandford (London, 1996).

The Football Association Coaching Book of Soccer Tactics and Skills, Charles Hughes. Queen Anne Press (London, 1986).

The Handbook of Soccer, Don Howe and Brian Scovell. Pelham Books (London, 1988).

The Football League 1888–1988, Bryon Butler. Macdonald Queen Anne Press (London, 1987).

Trevor Brooking's 100 Great British Footballers. Macdonald Queen Anne Press (London, 1988).

The Daily Telegraph Football Chronicle, Norman Barrett. Carlton Books (London, 1994).

Soccer Firsts, John Robinson. Guinness Superlatives Ltd. (Enfield, 1986).

Index